T0090481

NO WASTED MOVEMENT:
GROWING IN DISCOMFORT

JARED GIVENS

BALBOA.PRESS

A DIVISION OF HAY HOUSE

Balboa Press books may be ordered through booksellers or by contacting:

Balboa Press
A Division of Hay House
1663 Liberty Drive
Bloomington, IN 47403
www.balboapress.com
844-682-1282

Print information available on the last page.

Library of Congress Control Number: 2022913163
ISBN: 979-8-7652-3153-1 (sc)
ISBN: 979-8-7652-3155-5 (hc)
ISBN: 979-8-7652-3154-8 (e)

Balboa Press rev. date: 07/19/2022

CONTENTS

ACKNOWLEDGMENTS

First off, I would like to thank God for giving me the time to work on this book. I was not motivated all the time. I felt like I was not worthy enough to send a message. But what pushed me was my faith and consistency. Secondly, my family. My parents Walter and Monica Givens have supported me through every pursuit. My brother Philip kept me entertained for years and still does today. To my grandparents, aunts, uncles, and cousins, I love you all. Your relative is an author. To my friends from the Wichita Northwest class of 2020, I hope you are all doing well, chasing your dreams. I have also been blessed from the beginning with amazing coaches that showed me how to be a light in the community. Coach Marvin, thank you for introducing me to the game of football. To my high school coaching staff, I appreciate everything you did for me during my four years. For my readers, thank you again for picking up this book. You spent a portion of your time reading this and I am grateful for you. When I first started writing, I had no idea who my audience would be. It turns out, that this is not only for people in my age group and older. This is a message to my younger self too. I spent weeks feeling like this book would fail to reach people. Like I said in the beginning if this helped one person, I would be satisfied. This is my contribution to the community. I want to thank the people at Balboa Press for allowing me to share my vision and turn my idea into a reality. In conclusion, I want you, wherever you are in life, to make a change. I want you to become the best version of yourself. The days will not always be peaceful, but you become stronger by continuing. So continue. Grow in discomfort.

INTRODUCTION

How fast is life moving for you? Are you living in a constant state of worry or panic? Are you tossing and turning trying to find comfort in this life? Let me be the first or millionth to tell you not to worry. Easier said than done right? As humans, we naturally gravitate towards what is comfortable. If we face opposition, there is a voice in our heads telling us to quit. Instant gratification is the bandaid that we place on our scarred life in need of stitches. We look for validation outside our respective groups to make a move. Some of us had faith in people that hurt us. Maybe you used pain to propel you. Others might have pushed the pain deep down until it bubbles up like throwing mentos in Diet Coke. If you are in a season of climbing mountain after mountain, congratulations. The obstacles have a purpose, and maybe you have no idea what that purpose is. If you picked up this book, you are curious and searching for something meaningful. As a self-aware individual, you possess the hunger to add value to your environment. But what do you want to accomplish? Who are you right now, and who are you trying to be in the future? Hopefully, you do not feel trapped in an interrogation room as you read through these questions. Keep these in mind as you continue.

If you don't know who I am, my name is Jared Givens. I was born and raised in Wichita, Kansas. I graduated from Northwest High School in 2020. Yes, the year 2020. I got the idea of writing a book while in quarantine during my first year of college. Fortunately, I tested negative but my roommate tested positive. He was asymptomatic. This is not a book about coronavirus. Everyone has their opinions on it and that is not the message I am trying to convey. However, I am aware that I was not the only one that has changed since then. After months of uncertainty, I created routines that allowed me to get better physically, mentally, and spiritually. On July 1, 2021, I bought a journal from Walmart, and a couple of pens, and started writing consistently. I found that journaling helped me collect my thoughts, positive and negative. I set aside time to write. For the days I felt like nothing was going right, I practiced gratitude. This allowed me to check myself daily. Identifying the lacking areas in your life is not an exciting task. You might feel like you have done nothing but sabotage yourself. At the very least, you know what you need to work on. The crazy part is, that you are closer than you think. In the simplest of terms, your dream requires a large amount of time and energy. But it does not all have to be done at one time. The mistake is thinking that all work and no relaxation will produce instant results. Unfortunately, the distractions are growing each day. It seems like there is a new form of entertainment that stands in the way of our progress as dream chasers. The outside forces are not in our favor. Writing this book has been on my mind for well over a year now. I am not your typical author. I am fairly young but old enough to acknowledge everything that happens around me. Through years of playing sports and working with others, I felt like I needed to add value. If this book only reaches one person, then I will not be discouraged because that one person can make a huge difference.

Wherever you are in life, there is at least one thing you can improve upon. If you believe you have it all together and need no assistance, then you would not seek help or build relationships. You would go on about your day and never look back. As this world changes, we must change. I am not saying we become like the world, rather we become the best version of ourselves. Of course, that is different for everyone. We are not meant to live a life of misery, full of dark days. Will you have to live through dark times? Yes! The great part about that is everyone faces challenges on their journey. Contrary to what you might think, you are not alone. I wrote this book for those that feel isolated. It is hard to chase your purpose when countless activities are starving for your attention. In this book, you will gain knowledge about methods you can use on your path to greatness. To get to that next level you need a plan. If no one else sees what you see, you must keep your vision alive. You don't have to be understood to accomplish great things. The people close to you don't need to know your next move. Life will knock you down and continue to test you. When you take calculated risks you are already further than those who are not trying. Before you finish this book, I would like to say I appreciate the time you took to pick this up. Imagine what your life will look like if you apply just a few principles from this book. The truth is, you can read all the books in the world and not work to change your circumstances. You can watch all the videos that provide the steps to reach your goals but if you do nothing, you are just spinning your wheels. Get up and look in the mirror. Smile. You are alive today. You have a purpose. If you are willing to put in the work and keep an open mind, then you are ready. Picture your younger self looking at you. Make that person proud. So take notes, and read this by yourself, or with others. Let this not be an assignment, but a stepping stone for your growth. I wish you the best.

CHAPTER 1

JOURNEY

ourney. What do you think about when you see that word? Do you think about a mountain climber finally reaching the top, or do you think about a person crawling through the desert suffering from dehydration? You could be thinking about a time when you drove more than eight hours from one state to another. Whatever popped into your head is for you to keep. Due to your current state or the way you were raised, the word journey can trigger delight, sorrow, or have no meaning at all. From the time you were born to the present day, you have explored your options and resources. You communicated through crying or putting words together when you wanted to eat. Before you were strong enough to walk, you crawled. Before you were able to use the bathroom with no help, you trained. Within your first few years of life, you had to pick up a pen or pencil to print your name for the first time. After you mastered this task, it became muscle memory. Through exploration, you chose your favorite color, activities, and foods. Without your curiosity about adventure, you would find it hard to know what you are allergic to, or what you are not interested in. Most people are full of energy during the first eighteen years of their life. They get good grades, rarely miss a day, and they have big dreams. Then something bad happens. The desire to accomplish something slowly goes away. Why? The individual is more focused on the result than the process. The added pressure that comes with this mentality is unnecessary. Many people might say they want to be a millionaire or own a business. While the result is what most people care about, you must look within yourself. How are you growing in the process? Will you continue to put in the hours when the results are not present? What can you do to adjust your path? No matter how hard you try, you cannot predict the exact moment when you will see the seeds you planted grow into a fruit-bearing tree. But you can estimate where you will be if you stay on a consistent path. If your goal is to lose weight, then it might not be a great idea to stop by McDonald's for breakfast. If you desire to be smarter with your finances, it is a promising idea to track your spending through an app on your phone or computer. The results are only a product of the work you put in. Keyword "consistent." The world today is spending time and energy trying to pull you down the wrong paths. If you fail to watch your step, you might fall into the trap that is growing quicker by the day. So how do you start? You need direction. When you are traveling to an unfamiliar place, keeping a map is essential. Using landmarks can help you adjust to your environment. After all, you want to put yourself in the best position to win. Your dream exists in an unfamiliar place because you are not there yet. You might have an idea where it will take you, but it is not a guarantee. As mentioned before, you need direction. You need to know where you are going, even if it is new. As humans, we are naturally resistant to change. At the same time, we cry out for change when something does not go our way. An exercise that I practiced in high school that I still practice today is writing down my goals. I started identifying goals for the year and made the steps to reach them by a certain date. If you are anxious about the year, then you can break your list down into monthly checkpoints. If that is too much, then weekly and daily lists work just as well. The next step is placing what you wrote in a place where you can see it every day. I used to place mine on my door so when I left my room, it would be the first thing I saw. There is a certain level of accountability when you write something down. What needs to be done is on your mind. You no longer have to make impulsive decisions because you know where you want to be. If you need more clarification, spend time by yourself. Define your values and anything that does not line up with those values should be discarded from your life. The journey is about growing. Your past self will be competing with your current self. The behaviors you adopted in your earlier years will come back up. The lists are meant to keep you in check. This is not meant to be comfortable. The more uncomfortable you are, the greater the growth. When you get rid of these habits and influences in your life, you might feel like a part of you is missing. I have felt the same way. When you are on your way to what you believe is the top, you are going to have to cut some of that nonsense out. Think about the benefits in the long run, not the short term. With no action, the dream that you had in your mind for years will continue to be in your mind on your deathbed. We are not meant to stay the same and work jobs we do not like to pay bills in a location that is not optimal. Every time you win, even if it is small, takes you a step closer to that wild vision you possess. The power is in you. Everyone has skills and talents that can allow them to add value to this world. Some people spend their whole lives in a miserable state because they did not take the risks. I do not want you to become that person. You deserve to use the time and energy given to you to be great. If you have that voice in your head telling you that you can do more, listen to it. Your morals and values will be the compass, all you have to do is move forward. Embrace the challenges and push yourself. The majority of people only push themselves to their breaking point. What you need to do is push past your breaking point. Lifting weights is a perfect example. I started lifting weights during the winter of my freshman year in high school. I played football and ran track. My head football coach made all of us attend 6 AM weights. This was called 'zero hour'. For four days a week, there would be a workout. Mondays, Tuesdays, Thursdays, and Fridays were designated for lifting only. During the season, Wednesdays were yoga days followed by the film study. Attendance was mandatory and most of the team would show up. When I first started lifting, my form was ineffective. My shoulders and back would be tight before school. By the end of the season, we were maxing out on three compound lifts. If you are not familiar with these, we maxed out on squat, bench press, and hang clean. I was barely 140 pounds at the time, standing at five-foot-six inches. I ended up lifting my weight or lower on all three. After this day I was not satisfied. I looked at the upper-class students who were lifting three to four times what I was lifting. At first, I was discouraged because I was comparing myself to them. From this day on, I focused on my lifting technique and building muscle in the process. I started drinking protein shakes and lifting six days a week. My diet was still inconsistent, and my energy was not where I wanted it to be. After sophomore year, I saw a glimpse of my future results. I gained fifteen pounds and my maxes went up. Something in me told me that I can do better. I could lift more, be faster, and be a better teammate. I was lucky enough to have leaders in the class in front of me to be successful. They were the vocal leaders; I lead by example. The highlight of my day in high school was lifting. It still is to this day. Beginning the day with a workout sets the tone for the remaining tasks ahead. This is not only preparing, you for that day. Exercise in any form is testing your toughness physically and mentally. I love it. Years ago, when I walked into a gym, I would compare myself to the biggest guys no matter how old they looked. I was intimidated by the weight they were moving so effortlessly. Through my junior and senior years, I felt like I was built, but I kept focusing on other people. My ego told me to lift more because the guy on that machine is lifting more. Pushing through the pain and neglecting form got me nowhere. I was consistent but sometimes I worked harder and not smarter. By the time I graduated, I only missed one day of weights during my first year due to lower back pain. Through four years, I gained around fifty pounds and maintained a healthy physique. I am not sharing this to brag. Did I feel like quitting? Of course. I fell many times; the only difference is I got up and kept going. I kept showing up and I did extra. What I had planned rarely came to fruition. What I saw in the mirror was just an accumulation of all the steps I took before. The routine that I built early on helped me in numerous ways. Zero hour was at six o'clock every morning. Waking up just after five was not easy at first. But I knew if I wanted to become a better version of myself, I would have to wake up early and execute. After a few months, I started enjoying the work. If I ever failed to complete a certain movement, then I would seek help from my older teammates. My older teammates helped me grow physically and mentally. I had two decisions back then. The first was, to wake up, put in the hours, and lead by example. The second choice was quitting. I loved football at the time, I still love it now. So, I decided to step up and embrace the challenges ahead. All the conditioning, early mornings, and practices. There will be some growing pains, but that is a part of becoming the best version of yourself. You must embrace the challenges. Everyone gets the same twenty-four hours a day. If you want to be great, you have no choice but to work. While that might sound overwhelming in your head, it is the truth. The hardest part is starting. The second hardest part is staying consistent. As a student-athlete, I am lucky to have coaches and teammates around me to keep me accountable. But that is not the case for most people. One quality of a successful individual is integrity. Being honest to others is easy, being honest with yourself is harder. Millions of people want change, but few of them want to change. Fixing the bumps and bruises on the outside is a simple task. But evaluating your moves internally might just be the difference between average and great. What you do when no one is watching or when nothing is due is important. Where do you see yourself in the next year? How much money do you want to make at a certain age? Waiting for something miraculous to happen will not create the results you desire. Picture a lion in the desert. The lion sees a herd of antelope. Each antelope represents an opportunity. The herd is running effortlessly through the desert, they are in order. The lion waits for hours looking for the biggest one. But they all look similar. The sun is setting, the herd is gone. Nothing but the stars and sounds of hyenas in the distance. The lion, still in the same position gets up and walks back to his home hungry. Every opportunity to eat passed him by. He had no focus, no drive. He was exhausted from the previous day. He was afraid of failing. The truth is, he lost the battle against his mind. He was created to hunt and thrive in his environment. Unfortunately, his mentality was off. Does this sound like you? Stop procrastinating, waiting for the right moment to strike. There is no such thing as the right time. The longer you wait, the harder it is to find the next opportunity. More people will get the results that they put in the work for while you are stuck in the same place. Just like the lion. You should want to improve in every area of your life. This should not feel like a chore. The path to success is not a straight road. There are no shortcuts. You will doubt yourself. If you are not in the location or position, you want to be in then it is your responsibility to get there. The week between Christmas Day and New Year's Day is an interesting time. Most people are spending time with their families. Eating more and watching television. For some, it is a time of reflection. Looking back at the year and evaluating. You should not wait until the last few days of the year to evaluate yourself. Why not do it monthly, or daily? This does not take a large amount of time. Just take a few minutes to think about your day. Three things could have happened. You either got better, got worse, or did not change at all. As hard as it is, you cannot sugarcoat your situation. You are where you are today because of previous decisions. Habits both good and bad have placed you here. If you are satisfied with where you are at, then do not change. But if you are hungry for success, if you have dreams that scare you, then you must get better. It is okay to start small. Work on your dreams daily. Then stack those days one by one. Eventually, you will have a productive week, turned into a productive month. Take those months of laser-sharp focus and you will have a productive year. At the very least, six months of working on a new skill, managing your money, or building your business can put you further ahead. Remember, your dreams matter. This does not mean they matter to others. The people closest to you might doubt you for years until they finally see your results. On your way to the top, whatever that looks like for you, there will be those who speak positively about your life and those who are negative. What worked for me is ignoring both types and using that energy to move forward. The people that support lead you to complacency meaning you will not have the will to keep going because you are okay with where you are. The people that want to see you fail are insecure with themselves. They envy you because you are acting. Revealing your main plan to both types will throw you off course. The pressure is added now that more people expect you to reach that goal. Instead of sharing your dreams and goals with others, you should keep them to yourself. Write your goals down for the weeks and months. At the end of the day, these people are waiting for results. The haters will continue to envy, and the supporters will say congratulations. It is up to you and only you to stay accountable. They cannot lift the weights, budget the money, or sell the products for you. What they offer is their voices, their word. Do not let the support go to your head, do not let the hate pierce through your heart. Use both as fuel. You are not working to prove them wrong; you are working to prove yourself right. Imagine how the success will feel. Those late nights and early mornings changed you. They will call you an overnight success when you failed a few times. Your failures do not define you forever. When something is not working, you find a way to fix it. Everyone comes from diverse backgrounds. We grow up sitting in the backseat of our parents' cars. We start in a car seat facing backward when we are a few months old. Then we move on to the booster seat. Usually, before middle school, we are big enough to turn the airbag on in the front seat. From early childhood to young adulthood, we watch our families drive their cars. The sound of the windshield wipers on a rainy day, the sound of the turn signals, and the horn. They have helped you get to your events and appointments. You have gone through these years trusting them behind the wheel. At the time you were the passenger. At some point, you decided to learn how to drive. You might have practiced in an empty parking lot or drove downtown and parallel parked. Either way, you took the steps to become a successful driver. Everything you learned in driving school you applied to life behind the wheel. You have been the driver of your own life. Whether you accept that role or not is up to you. Eventually, you will have to live on your own, make money on your own, and take care of yourself. No one is going to hold your hand on your journey. Some assistance is necessary, but you need the experience. This does not mean you are thrown in the fire, and you must fight your way out. No. This means through trial and error you figure out what works best for you. If that method brings you the results you want, then you find ways to optimize it. You make the process quicker, and more efficient. Start a new routine today. Figure out what is holding you back from reaching your full potential. One issue I dealt with was my sleeping schedule. I would have enough energy to get work done within the first half of the day by energy tanked in the afternoon. The root of my problem was my screen time and my horrible time management when it came to finishing homework. Instead of going through the day with excitement, it was more like dragging my feet. So, I checked my screen time on my phone. I was spending over eight hours on social media and streaming services. This time could have been used to study or rest. I put a limit on the amount of time I spent on my phone. Within the first week, I got better sleep and finished my homework hours before bed. This might seem like a small edit in my original routine, but it worked. One slight change allowed me to be more productive. Imagine how great you could be with just a few slight changes in your daily routine. Every change will give you a different result than before. When you stick to this routine of constant improvement you will soon see the results and appreciate the work you have done. But this is a continuous cycle. First, find something that you need to work on. For example, if it is something as simple as your sleep schedule, then determine the root cause. If you are on your phone or computer right before bed, then you should replace that activity with something beneficial. You could read a book, meditate, or do yoga. These are light activities that can help you fall asleep faster with a clear mind. After implementing this change, you should work to optimize your routine. Find what works best for you and your situation. What might work for your friends and family might not work for you. Remember, everybody has a different journey. Comparing yourself to others will get you nowhere. Picking up a new hobby or replacing a negative behavior with positive behavior is not easy. This is where the optimization comes in. Start where you are now. Do not wait. If you make one change today, then you are already ahead of those who are waiting around for some motivation. Uncertainty comes with change. You will start to question yourself. You will wonder if the path you take will be worth your time. Truthfully, it is. A routine is not a life sentence. You are not chained to your routine because you have the power to upgrade it. We are surrounded by growth. We live in an age of innovation through technology. Everything moves at a faster rate than before. Apple upgrades the iPhone yearly. Roads are under construction everywhere. Buildings are going up in small cities. Ask yourself this question. People upgrade their phones, cars, and even houses. What is stopping you from upgrading your life? Is it your fear of failure? Is it your insecurities? Or you feel like you are no longer in control. Years go by quickly. Some people wait for the calendar to say January 1st to do something about their situation. Instead of making a list of overwhelming resolutions, break them down into months. Then figure out what steps you must take weekly to reach the monthly goals. When I was in elementary, over the summers, my mom would sign my brother and me up for the summer reading program. My brother and I hated it. The requirement was thirty minutes of reading every day. You would think that thirty minutes was such a brief time for a child who is too busy playing sports and enjoying the weather. No. What felt like an eternity was simply thirty minutes committed to reading a book. We got the weekends off from reading. We each had a worksheet we filled in after reading. Five days a week, two and a half hours of reading. Every week we would stop by the library to turn in our sheets. There was a different theme each year, but the rewards were the same. If you read a certain number of hours, you could earn a coupon for a personal pan pizza at Pizza Hut. More hours would get you a Taco Bell coupon and a bookmark. With the worksheets turned in, you can enter a drawing for prizes like tickets to the movies, t-shirts, books, and more. Even though I picked out the books I wanted to read, I still felt like it was forced. Thank goodness for the incentives or I would have lost the desire to read. My brother also enjoyed the fruits of his labor through pizza and tacos. Eventually, it did not feel forced. The prizes did not matter as much, but the information I retained from each book was meaningful. I tried reading new genres and I found out what I liked to read. The summer was around ten to eleven weeks long before school started again. Apart from vacations, I spent around twenty to thirty total hours reading the whole summer. Most of that time I was complaining and resisting, which was wrong. I should have embraced the challenge of improving my reading skills and comprehension. But as a kid, a break from school felt more comfortable. Swimming every day at our neighborhood pool sounded more exciting than sitting on a couch with a book. As mentioned before, the incentives gave me something to chase after positively. Was I a little bit greedy back then? Yes. But the small wins like four mini slices of pizza kept me going. That is what you need to do in your life. Do not overthink the steps. All you need to do is take the first step, then the second, then the third. I started the summer reading only thirty minutes a day, then it turned into two thirty-minute sessions a day. When I found books I enjoyed, I would go back to the same authors to read their next pieces of work. It was exciting because I only read from a few authors. Then I focused on one genre at a time and found more books to read from more authors. This cycle continued throughout most of high school as well. My time was limited due to football, but I found a way. I did not make my goals clear about reading; I just read. If I put a limit on how many books, then I would have stopped a long time ago. The difference between then and now is the external rewards versus the internal rewards. The external rewards were coupons, t-shirts, and other prizes. The internal rewards were the words from another author, the information from each book, and the feeling of accomplishment after finishing. It was not about the level I was reading at before the new school year, it was about what I learned in the process. You need to create incentives for yourself both internally and externally. Think about where you could be if you stick with it. You may not be living around understanding and caring people, but you must push through. Imagine your health in six months if you keep going to the gym, making your meals, and stop eating fast food. Imagine your bank account if you stop buying unnecessary products to look successful around people who do not support you. Where will you be if you stay consistent? A better place. You might not reach that big dream yet, but you will be that much closer. Where will you be if you quit? Nowhere. The same place or worse. Understand that sometimes you will have to clap for yourself. You will have to work when you do not feel like it. Like years ago, I did not feel like reading, but I did it anyway. I did not want to lift weights or condition, but I did it anyway. I did not want to do extra, but I did it anyway. The rewards were worth the risks. I never woke up stronger, I worked for it. I never liked books until I tracked my reading. Create the incentives and remember them. These will push you when you cannot see hope. When your back is against the wall, you can lean on the benefits of suffering. Suffering is not a terrible thing. No one is holding your hand every single step of the way. You might have to win in the dark and lose in the dark to dominate in the light. Pilots train for months to be ready to get people from point A to B. They face turbulence in the air all the time. But they get through it by taking control and staying calm. You are the pilot of your life, and even if you nosedived a couple of times, you still could get back up. Appreciate where you are right now in this moment. Be grateful for what you have. Now figure out what you want for yourself. You should know by now that success is not given to you, it is earned. Believe in your dreams even if you are by yourself. These are your goals, your dreams, it does not matter who supports them or not. Reject the disease of mediocrity and self-pity. Embrace the grind, the ugly stages, and the pretty stages. You do not need an audience, focus on yourself. Picture yourself in the future. Will the future version of yourself be proud of the hours you are putting in or will that person be disgusted? It is up to you. Take the steps today to prepare you for tomorrow. Everyone takes a different path to their version of success. Some make it in a year, others in five years. You are on your timeline, not theirs. During your school days, were you ever assigned a big project? Maybe it was for science or history class. Remember how you felt when you finished the project. Did you get a good grade on it? If not, that is okay because it is in the past. Whether you got an A or an F, you had to finish that project at the said deadline. You either put in the work or you did not. The deadline was out of your control. But you are here now, years later with more knowledge and experience. In life, you are your biggest project. Maybe you play sports, where you are judged on your performance. You might be close to getting a raise or promotion at your job based on your results. When you are working on yourself, there are no deadlines. No one is in your ear telling you to move. You can set your deadlines. Being on your own time can present great results or none. If you procrastinate, then you are holding yourself back. Other people might stand in your way, but do not stand in your way. It is okay if you do not have everything figured out. All you need to do is take the first step. You did not learn how to walk by sprinting first, you put one foot in front of the other and kept going. Did you fall sometimes? Yes. But you got up also. Another part of the journey is unpredictable seasons. I am from Wichita, Kansas. The meteorologists here do their best job to predict the weather. But sometimes the result is not what they expected. Depending on where you are in the state, it could be mild one day and snow the next day. Or it could be below thirty degrees and get above seventy on the same day. The predictions are not one hundred percent accurate every week. However, there is technology and resources that help provide the most accurate weather predictions everywhere. When you are working to grow into the person you want to be, you will face some unpredictable seasons. You might lose money, friends, and support from your family. Remember who you are doing this for, yourself. There is nothing wrong with putting yourself first. After all, it is your journey, your story. You have the decision every day you wake up to choose your dreams. Nothing great is ever accomplished without some form of resistance. For example, an artist might release two albums of sixteen songs each, but all it takes is that one song to reach the top of the charts. A player might be injured for two seasons, go through rehab, and suddenly they are putting up all-star stats and win an MVP award. That is the beauty of the journey. You learn a lot about yourself. You find out what works and what does not. The wins and losses matter but do not get stuck in those moments. Keep in mind, that everyone takes a different path. Do not take your eyes off the road looking at someone else. Embrace the challenges as they will make you stronger and equip you with more knowledge. Start a new routine, and new methods to get to that next level. Upgrade the routine to make your steps as effective as possible. When you stick to this routine daily, it turns into a weekly routine. Soon it will be monthly and hopefully yearly if you stay consistent. After those hours you put in, create an incentive or a reward. Remember how you benefit from acting and not waiting. This is earned not given. If you wanted to be average, then you would not feel the need to change. At some point, you got tired of making the same mistakes, entertaining the same habits, and hurting your personal growth. The journey is meant to shape you, and mold you into the person you want to be. This does not happen by accident. The path is intentional work, and it will get messy sometimes. You do not become strong without lifting the heavy weights, physically and figuratively. The biggest project you will ever work on is yourself. You will either look back with pride or disgust. As you know, no one is setting the deadlines for you to upgrade your life. The longer you wait, the harder it might be to get better. You have the power; you have the ability. Believe in yourself. This is a long road, and you might feel like you already made it. Get that out of your head. Always improve, and keep on learning. This is your life.

CHAPTER 2

COMFORT ZONE

Not all of us come from traditional families. Some of you come from broken families, and some of you are adopted. You might have been raised by your grandparents or other relatives. Most parents and legal guardians want the best for the child they are taking care of. This involves the responsibility of making the child or children as comfortable as possible. While this is important in the first few years of life, it must be reduced as they get older. I am not here to teach you how to parent if you are one. The comfort zone can be a lonely place. You stay in the same place, with the same people, doing the same activities continually. This is a tough cycle to get away from. When a person graduates high school, they are presented with a few decisions. One of them is college, the next is the workforce, and another might be joining the military. If there is a family business, then maybe they stay and continue the legacy of the people before them. What I am going to highlight is college. When you move to a college where most of your friends are going, it is easier to keep that bond with your circle. After all, you have followed each other to the same place to make more memories. On the other side, there is uncertainty. When you move to an institution out of state or somewhere different than your friends, you are already stepping outside your comfort zone. Now you have to build new relationships with people you have never met. If you are used to home-cooked meals, well, now you have to shop for yourself or eat what the school provides. The school could be in a small town while you came from a big city or the opposite. Whether you like it or not, you must adapt to your environment. You cannot succeed by staying in one place mentally and physically. Today, the world has provided many outlets that are loaded with instant gratification. If you are not familiar with what instant gratification is, then think about your most liked post on Instagram. How did that make you feel? Think about that time you ordered food and it arrived within ten minutes. You got exactly what you wanted in the short term, by exhausting little to no effort at all. The dopamine rush you got made you crave it more. The fact that you can reasonably get anything you want instantly is a factor that holds you back. The constant scrolling, looking for the next rush, the next trend to impress others. We have apps for delivering food and other products. We have apps that allow you to pick your potential partner. You get what you want when you want it. This age of technology has some positive and negative effects. The amount of time you spend on your phone could be used to get closer to your goals. One great part about what we have today is the process of creating the content the way you want. Obviously, within the rules and regulations of the medium used. You can advertise your business at any time. Virtually, you can leave an impact on others. But we are meant for more than a social media presence. If you are always comfortable you will not grow. So many people complain about not having enough time to get things done. The days might drag on because you are stuck at the office with a pile of paperwork. Other days might go by so fast that you forget the month is over and you have made no progress. What worked for me in the past, that still works today is tracking my screen time. In the settings app on your phone, there should be a section that shows how much time you spend on every app you open throughout the day. The option to set app limits is there too. Looking at how you spend your time is humbling. This is good. You should check yourself when you feel like you are going nowhere. When I first checked my screen time, I was averaging six to seven hours on social media alone. This is time I could have spent learning a new skill or meeting new people. When you look at how you are spending your time, you start to realize how much you have wasted. This is okay. You are aware now, which is farther than most people. The attempts are being made to snap yourself out of the cycle. We like patterns and regularity. As long as we know what will happen next, we have nothing to worry about. That is one reason why we eat the way we do, watch the shows we love, and connect with people that fit the pattern. I am challenging you to challenge yourself. For seven days, track your screen time. Find out what apps you use the most, then cut back on what is not benefiting you. Try to lower your screen time each day. At the end of the seven days, you should have an average. This is your new benchmark. Use this going forward. If you go over the time, that is okay. If you are under, great. After this exercise, you are more inclined to watch how you spend your time. You do not have to put every move you make under a microscope, that will drive you crazy. Simply being mindful of where you exert your energy is enough. Hopefully, you will find that you do not need to scroll through social media as much as you think. Replacing old habits with new ones can spark a new fire within you. You do not look at tasks you have to complete as obstacles. Now that you have freed the time needed to get those done, you are not as anxious as before. In my experience, I am more motivated to attack the tasks I used to put off. You receive a sense of accomplishment when you use your time wisely. One step forward is better than staying stagnant. Imagine where you could be if you keep inching towards the future you want. Sometimes, your comfort zone includes people that have done nothing to reach their goals. These people work all week at dead-end jobs and go to the clubs every weekend. This type of person hates their job, but they stay there because it pays the bills. They are stuck in an endless loop of overindulgence. This person is negative and finds the problem in every situation. You already have an idea of what they are going to say before they say it. Due to the demands at work and unnecessary clubbing, they have not carved out time to build something. No time is devoted to their dreams. This person used to be full of ambition and positivity. Somewhere along the road, they lost their fire. You see how much this person has changed over the years, yet you still call them your friend. The next point is that some people that reside in your comfort zone are temporary. Notice how I did not say all people. I am specifically calling out that friend or group of friends that are doing nothing with their lives. The ones that fail to take ownership of their actions that got them where they are today. One of the hardest parts about stepping outside your comfort zone is leaving those you care about. The years of memories in school or at the last job you worked at might begin to resurface. Talking about the past is not a bad thing, but you do not live there anymore. Whatever happened, happened. What are you doing moving forward? If you feel like you are outgrowing your environment, you must move. It does not have to be out of the city or state. Today it is easy to become a product of your environment, but if you are self-aware, you know that you must grow. When you were a child, how did you pick an ice cream flavor? Maybe you chose off of the memory of similar tastes. Maybe your mom or dad chose the flavor for you. Understand that the ice cream shop or stand was unchartered territory for you. It was a place you have never been before. You were guided to a certain point and then started making decisions yourself. Maybe you tried chocolate and vanilla, but you saw that there were more flavors. Birthday cake, strawberry, chocolate chip cookie dough. You had the opportunity to expand your palate. This is life, except you may or may not be in an ice cream shop every week. The world presents you with millions of options in every area of your life. In your comfort zone, it is like putting on a blindfold. Your eyes are not open to new opportunities because you are afraid of what you might lose. Forget about what you can lose, picture what you can gain. The experience is priceless. If nothing else, you know what you can get better at and what you are great at. But how will you know if you do not try? If you have been on self-improvement for a while then you know that it can change those around you. They notice something different in the way you walk and talk. In the beginning, a part of them thought you would never accomplish what you said. Others might have been supporters from the start. No matter what you do, you will have haters and supporters. Two sides of the same coin. The positive voices will convince you that you have done enough. The negative voices will convince you that you have done nothing. When I receive words from both sides, I take them with a grain of salt. I acknowledge and thank those that continue to support me, but there is still work to be done. I take the negative words and turn them into fuel for the next mission. No hard feelings, just execution of what is in front of me. This is a challenge because it is easy to get caught up in what other people say. Adopt the new mentality that no matter what they say, you continue to work. In addition to this, if you do decide to leave this environment, then you need to build relationships with others. In the simplest of terms, you need to find people with similar interests. Whatever you are interested in, there will be people actively working in the same field. You never know when you might need these people. Not to say that you are using them for what they can give you, it is mutually beneficial. This is when you get to evaluate your current circle and update it. You do not have to be stuck with your current friends. At the same time, you do not have to be best friends with everybody you meet. As much as it is good to be self-sufficient in most areas, you need a support system. We need people to be there when we are not feeling our best. These individuals push us and remind us who we are when we get lost in our failures. The same actions are applied when people in your circle need a boost. As a determined individual, you deserve to receive the same energy that you give to others. If you never leave your comfort zone, you are depriving your future self of key relationships. I used to believe that all I needed was my friends from school, church, and sports. The truth is, those relationships while still meaningful, have gotten me nowhere. Think about it, how many friends from high school are you consistently in contact with today? If you have not graduated high school yet, then think of the friends you met in middle school. How many of them are at the same school you are at? Is your circle the same as it was four years ago, or eight years ago? If it is then you need to change it now. As soon as possible. I am calling you out, and I am calling myself out. In our younger years, we fall victim to the opinions of others. Social media does not make this any easier. We compare ourselves to our closest friends. We ask them if they like what we are wearing, what we bought, what we drive, and where we live. As hard as it is, their opinions good or bad will not get you to where you want to be. You will forever be seeking validation from everyone but yourself. How do you feel? If you cannot think for yourself, then the process of growing gets delayed. Imagine you and your friends are all overweight. Every time you hang out, you play video games, watch movies, and go out to eat. At this time you are not monitoring your calories and the only workout you get is walking from your car to the restaurant. After a year of hanging out with your friends, you start to feel sluggish and depressed. You used to have energy. You used to be full of life. Each day you are scrolling through social media and you see people in the gym with toned bodies. Now you are at war with yourself. Something inside of you is telling you that you should lose weight and see your friends less often. Another part of you is attached to the good times you have had up to this point; you do not want to abandon your friends. But you realize how staying in this restful environment can affect your health later on in life. So you decide to lose weight and eat healthier. Years of avoiding exercise and regularly consuming unhealthy meals have added up. The best thing you can do right now is to take small steps. If you have the money to buy a membership, you do so. To save money you learn how to cook healthy meals for weight loss. Months pass and you have stayed consistent, yet your friends are still in the same place. One year passes by and they have not changed their life. You ask yourself; "What is the difference between me and them?" The difference is that you stepped outside your comfort zone. You saw the unhealthy lifestyle that you were living and decided to fix that. There is a small level of guilt when you decide to leave your old habits. It is that same voice inside of you that fears the unexplored territory. From what I have experienced, the journey is much more exciting when your values get challenged. When you are up against the wall and there is nowhere else to go but forward; that is the true meaning of leaving your comfort zone. Seek discomfort. The rewards you want are there, they exist. Have faith in your abilities, you are not meant to be hidden from the world. You have a purpose.

CHAPTER 3

PURPOSE

I n the conclusion of the last chapter, I told you that you have a purpose. A lack of purpose or a lack of even feeling useful can diminish your ambition. If you feel like you are not useful, then there is no drive to be better. When you ignore what you are destined for, you leave everything on the table. People who refuse to chase their purpose in life end up working jobs they hate. The passion they had for x,y, and z slowly disappeared. This was a gradual change, not instant. I want you to define what the end looks like to you. The end is your successful life, your legacy. What does it look like? What does it feel like? Defining what the end looks like will give you some clarity from the beginning. This will give you an idea of how to start. Write it down. Make it visible. This is your vision. Take this exercise seriously. This is not the regular online survey that tells you where you fit in society. Writing your vision down with as much detail as possible will help. There should be a picture in your mind. Visualization is powerful. This is like getting a sneak peek of the future. Everything you imagined, everything you dreamed of is coming to fruition. To fully embrace your purpose, you need to establish a growth mindset. Fixed thinking will hold you back. A growth mindset is a belief that through hard work and dedication, an individual can accomplish anything. The talents and skills that you have can be developed over time. Nobody is born a professional. As a one-month-old, you cannot dunk a basketball, play the piano, or paint a mural. The exposure to multiple outlets as a child and young adult has given you those skills. It was through continuous efforts to get better at what you liked. So what does this look like? Is this a destination or a constant pursuit? We must first look at it from different perspectives. In the process of writing this chapter, I emailed a few of the coaches and teachers I had in the past. I asked two questions. The first is, "what does the word *purpose* mean to you?" The second is, "how does one find purpose in life?" Coach Martin, my high school football coach said that it is the actions we take to attain a certain goal or objective. The "why" is the driving force. To become a high school coach, he worked hard and refused to fail. One finds their purpose through living life to the fullest and experiencing new things. He decided to become a coach because his high school coach took an interest in him. As a result, he wanted to give back the gift he received. He played college football so he could network with people in that area. My English teacher Dr. Minerva had similar answers. She said that it is the 'why' in any situation. Why certain actions and choices are made. In her words, purpose in life is found by knowing yourself. One way to find out what fulfills you is by identifying your strengths and interests. Another interesting point is found in failure. You try something, if it does not fit you right, then you learn from that. When she finished college, she had no idea of what she was going to do. There is uncertainty between the ages of eighteen and twenty-four because you are trying to make big decisions. She moved to western Massachusetts and attended UMass for grad school. In a year, she met tons of incredible people, worked different jobs, and evaluated her options. By the age of twenty-three, she applied to grad school at Indiana University in Bloomington. She was a teaching assistant, so she got to see both sides of education. As a half-student, half-teacher she found out she loved working with students. Since then she has been an English teacher leading different classes at different levels. The individuals I contacted have been gracious enough to share a part of their stories. I am thankful to have had committed teachers and coaches in my earlier years. The common theme here is the 'why.' Most people do not define the why until they reach a certain level of success. This does not have to be identified in the beginning but it should be before a goal is reached. You must ask yourself who you are doing this for and why you are doing it. Similar to your vision, it is important to write this down. This is something you can always come back to when you face adversity. If you have no foundation in anything, make this your foundation. Make this your mission. Your strengths and interests will only get you closer to your purpose. How do you know what you are good at? Through trial and error. If you never attempt to find yourself, then it will be harder to live out your vision. Conversely, some believe that life has no purpose. They are conditioned to fit old standards of living. We are only taught to get good grades and get a job with security. If we want to get married, we find a partner as fast as possible. We are afraid of being too late compared to our friends or family members. We attempt to please those around us as a defense mechanism. Our dreams are sacrificed for a share of short-lived popularity. Why are we so afraid to put ourselves first? Maybe our circle tries to pull us down. Our friends see our success and envy starts to grow. The world offers pleasure more than purpose. Putting yourself first does not mean being narcissistic. There are two sides to this. One side is the doormat. Everyone walks on this individual. They are used for their kindness and attention. People prey on this person because of their availability and generosity. This person puts everyone else before themselves even if it means they get nothing in return. There is no sense of entitlement. The other side is narcissism. On this side, there is a high level of selfishness that can be detrimental if this individual wants to be a long-term success. This person lacks empathy and everyone they come in contact with is inferior. If you have ever been on a sports team, worked on a group project, or collaborated with coworkers these two types of people exist. In addition to this, there are people in the middle and those that are closer to each side. Now you have a combination of personalities on one team. Believe it or not, all of these individuals have a part to play. There is a function for every part. The energy might be off, but it can be channeled. Wherever you are on the spectrum, there is a place for you. Do not believe the lie that you add no value to your current environment. Do not feed into the voices that tell you that you are just another number. Understand that self-doubt is a part of the process. I go back to the lifting example in my life. When I first started, I doubted myself. My form was not all the way correct. I did hurt my back multiple times. The warm-up stretches that I did were not taken seriously. It was when I took the time to learn. Instead of having a fixed mindset thinking I was not good at this, I chose to grow. After putting my body under tons of stress, I turned to reliable videos and articles. I did my research. My search history consisted of 'how to bench properly' and 'how to prevent injury while squatting.' Soon after, I looked up the proper diet for bulking. Bulking is what it sounds like, gaining weight. There is the clean bulk and the dirty bulk. A clean bulk includes healthy vegetables, fruits, meats, and carbs. A dirty bulk is essentially eating everything in sight without tracking calories. Sort of like eating fast food and whatever the person craves. I chose the clean bulk. After being mindful of what I ate, I ended up gaining forty pounds over four years. I lifted five to six times a week. When I was able to drive, I woke up early on weekends and formed a routine. Starting my day with a workout set me up for success. It did not matter how early I started, I just wanted to get it done before noon. On occasion, I would lift in the afternoon. The best part was, that I knew my 'why.' I did it for myself. The outside validation was nice for a while. But I did not let that take my eyes off the goals I set for myself. With every goal reached, I set new ones. The results did not appear by accident. I spent days in the dark, meaning I did certain things that no one saw. I was not working for an audience, I was working for my future self. You should do the same. Do not be alarmed by the intense call to action. For example, I did not jump to lifting heavier weights without first getting the form down. I did not consume protein shakes without first evaluating the brands. I did push-ups before I could bench. The same should be applied to your next move. Just because you have lofty goals does not mean you have to take extreme steps. Gradual steps are still steps. You are closer than you think. If it helps, you are closer than most. Do not let that go to your head though. There is work to be done. Set aside some time to think about the next step, then take the next step. Easier said than done right? Well, I want you to know that it is possible. You are not too early, you are not too late. As long as you have a pulse, you have the twenty-four hours given to you to chase your definition of greatness. I believed in what I did. You must believe in your abilities even if you are a beginner. The truth is every professional starts as a beginner. Working on yourself is scary at first, but it is also exciting. The lacking areas start to become more visible. If I were to train my chest and back every time I go to the gym but I fail to train my lower body, then I will look disproportionate. Similarly, you need to work on every area. The amount of time and energy does not have to be equally distributed. However, you need to make a conscious effort. Anything and everything can be improved. But do not get lost in the constricting details. I can say from experience, that trying to control everything will leave you feeling unfulfilled. The dissatisfaction will cause you to revert to the familiar habits that returned no progress. One common phrase that I have heard from previous employers, coaches, and teachers is "control what you can control." Everyone loves to be in control. The ability to do what you want when you want is something we can take for granted. I appreciate the person that said that there are three things one can control. The first is attitude, effort, and actions. All alarms come with some sort of snooze option. I like to think that this is a test. You set yourself up for discomfort, which is good. When the sound goes off it is human nature to ignore or press snooze. You are in charge of how you react. One little action can compound into great results or mediocre results. The choice is yours. If you wake up on time, you are more likely to execute your responsibilities for the day. When you do the opposite, it is like you are piling the work that needs to be done that day onto the next day. Keep repeating this cycle and you will be in the hole. It will be an uphill battle. At some point, you will ask yourself who is to blame. First, you had a poor attitude, then your actions were affected. As a result, your effort was below average. This produced little to no gains. However, if you do decide to immediately wake up without question, you are conditioning yourself. You are making the effort to be uncomfortable at the beginning of every day. In due time, this will become natural. When the months add up to years, it will be hard to remember a time when you did not wake up early. You will look at the person you were before and be appreciative of the new position. When you make these decisions for yourself and venture into the unfamiliar, there is fear. Before you take the first step, you wonder what people will think. Will your family support you? What if you lose all of your friends? What will people think? You are trying to back out last minute. If you could find enough excuses, then maybe you do not have to go through with this. If enough people have no belief in you, then maybe you do not need to change. Maybe this work is pointless. If you fail to accomplish your dreams will you still pursue them or quit? All of the outside factors start to creep in. If you start on Monday instead of Friday then you can have the weekend to think about it. No. If this, if that. Naturally, you are going to try to finesse your way to success by avoiding adversity. Adversity is a guide. Without it, you learn nothing. Every successful team that has accumulated many championships over many years started the season 0-0. No wins, no losses. The front office and coaches did their jobs by recruiting the best pieces to put the team in the best position to win. In the same way, you must build yourself. You will not be an immediate success. But you can speed up the process by recruiting the right parts of your identity to win. Fear will put pressure on you that seems unbearable. This is not for the weak. Those who are weak now will learn how to be strong through exposure. The highs and lows. Like a professional team, there are winning seasons and losing seasons. After a regular season of winning, the playoffs come. Depending on the sport, it is either a series or a one-and-done situation. Either way, no team wants to be down two or three losses. Certainly, no team wants to be out in the first round. Another part about your purpose that you need to understand is your competition. If you get lost in the comparing game, you will not be efficient. You are your competition. The battle starts when you wake up. What you eat, what you watch, and your beliefs are all factors. Of course, you will compete with others for a higher position. This is a part of life that the world is trying to eliminate. You should love to compete, especially against yourself. When you conquer the thoughts in your mind, the feeling is exhilarating. The hunger starts to grow, now you cannot wait to put in the work because you have seen some results. When you can beat the person in the mirror, there is more confidence to beat anyone that comes against you. The preparation builds confidence. When you believe in yourself regardless of the situation, you are powerful. One word that gets thrown around is accountability. There is a clear-cut definition for some, and others just ignore the importance. An accountable person takes responsibility for all of their actions. Accountability is the same shared value in an organization that allows people to be checked. Being able to hold someone to ethical standards is vital. Every organization is different. On your way up you will need partners, real friends that keep you accountable. I am not talking about friends that are sugar-coating the facts when you face resistance. You need people that are going to uplift and call you out. These people know what you are after. In a solid group, the relationships are mutual. Everyone benefits and provides value. This group does not have to be large. You are not an NFL coach trying to use a 53-man roster. Start small. Choose one or two, accountability partners. Preferably those that live in your city; people that you can meet up with. The trust is built the more times you meet. This can be once a week, a month, or quarterly. You do not have to share every detail of the moves you make with them either. But they do need to know what is working and what is not. Today it is easier to find what you are looking for due to social media and business apps. If you are not too reliant on technology, then you can go out and network. Go to events that interest you, seminars, or even the gym. You are in charge of how big or small your circle is. The key is to hold yourself accountable first, then include others. This relationship you will have is not like that of a parent. Picture yourself at the bowling alley. The bowling ball represents the actions and approaches you take. In life, you will find yourself in the gutter. Maybe you need to change your approach and speed. Your accountability partners are the bumpers. The pins are the barriers that are keeping you in the same place. When you get too close to the gutter, your partners are there to help. You do not desperately need them, but at least you know you have that option. We are meant to grow in community, not in isolation. In the beginning stages of the pandemic, we were advised to stay indoors. This was easy for some and harder for others. After two years of dealing with this, places are opening up.There are different ways to interact safely. Part of finding your purpose is finding your community. It is like you are working for something bigger than yourself while working on yourself. The value you provide for the world will give you fulfillment. Simultaneously, you should put your goals first. When you are firing on all cylinders, it will feel like there is no choice but to contribute to the community. At this point, it will not feel forced because you are passionate. Very few people get the opportunity to do what they love while getting paid. What outsiders fail to realize is that they began doing it for themselves. They were new to their passions and received no commission. They just had pure love for the activity. Remember, you get exactly what you work for. If you want clean teeth, then you would not forget to use toothpaste and only mouthwash. Those on a diet are not going to be able to exercise well if they are sleep-deprived. Everyone can target their strengths. If everyone did what they were great at but neglected their weaknesses, there would be wasted potential in many communities. Neglecting your weaknesses will not make them disappear. Using your time to constantly work on yourself despite your current circumstances is rewarding. A friend I had in high school named Louie is a passionate individual that comes to mind. His interests at the time were graphic design, clothing, and video production. He had some decisions to make. Would he specialize in one area or attempt to be above average in each one? He ended up using his time on each one. He created content like digital sports cards for athletes, training videos, and logos. It was only after he became seasoned in graphic design that he started his clothing brand. His initials are LA so he called it LA Productions. He sold hoodies, sweatpants, sweaters, and beanies. The greatest challenge for him was starting. Figuring out where to start can be a discouraging process. Louie kept going. He knew that he had to take some risks and make some sacrifices to level up. I was amazed at how fast he grew within the school. His friends and family supported him. His inner circle was there along the way. I started to see more people wear his clothing not only in school but in public too. At an age where most are focused on what others are doing, Louie channeled his energy into his brand. He inspired me to go after what I want in life. I enjoy watching people succeed, especially those close to me. I would like you to do the same. Do not get lost in what everyone else is doing. If you want to live like everyone else, then you do not need to change. You are perfect just the way you are. Right? I am not saying you should not be confident. You need to be. A lack of belief in what you are doing will always produce mediocre results. Whether you like it or not, you need to be completely bought in. Dipping your toe in the water is not going to cut it. Believe me, I have tried. The conditions will not always be in your favor. The more they are not in your favor, the more you grow. Sure, when you jump in a pool there is that initial shock. The feeling is terrible for ten seconds, and then your body adapts. You start to swim. The waves never stop. You explore what is not comfortable. But you believe in what you are doing. After swimming in this pool, you check out other pools. The water does not scare you because you are prepared to win. You have more confidence. Now you are on the high dive of life ready to make waves in your community. In this chapter, I gave you prompts to write your vision down. Knowing where you want to go is extremely important. Having no sense of direction can get you into undesirable places. Even if the end seems far for you, the work you do today can get you one step closer. For some, it is making a conscious effort to change one thing, then two, then three. Once one area is strong, you focus on the next one that needs attention. Have faith in yourself. You are in control of yourself. Like I mentioned before, control what you can control. This will relieve some of the stress that comes from wanting that power over every little thing in your life. You do not need to create a figurative pile of work. Finding your purpose requires doing what is in front of you. So do it. Do one push-up, write one song, eat one healthy meal, then increase accordingly. We like to overcomplicate our dreams. Yes, it is a big task. But the steps are simple. The execution however is the toughest part. I am convinced that this world is full of extraordinary people that are discouraged. Keep it simple. Go after what you want. Find your purpose. When you find it, never stop improving.

CHAPTER 4

CULTURE

North, east, south, west. Rich, middle-class, poor, homeless. Two parents, single-parent, grandparent, and foster parents. Black, White, Latino, Asian, Pacific Islander. Fill in the blank. Some of us have fair skin. In the summer we need more sunscreen than others. Some of us have darker skin. Sometimes we get more attention than others. Maybe our family is torn because our wealthy uncle has no intention of passing down his estate. Maybe we are pressured into fitting into the life that our family wants for us without considering our feelings. We want to live a better life. Some of us are immigrants with dreams. What can we accomplish in this country, in this world? How come our religion is judged by that religion? Nobody is wrong, right? If they just walked in my shoes maybe they could be more empathetic. A man named Daniel is on the beach standing across from his brother Greg. Greg grabs a stick and draws a six in the sand. But Daniel sees the number nine. No one is incorrect. There is just a different lens being used, a different perspective. If Daniel walked over to Greg's side then he would see that the number is six. But only from Greg's point of view. The same is true when Greg walks over to Daniel's side. So what do you do with this information? Well, let's begin by defining culture for what it truly is.

Culture is a term that covers social norms, beliefs, traditions, and how people operate in society. When you think of Chick-Fil-A, you think of the customer service. Every employee has a smile on their face and they end each interaction with the phrase "my pleasure." They lead by serving others. One can argue that every establishment that serves food practices servant leadership because it's their job. But the attitude, the consideration that separates this place from others. Within the first few minutes of stepping in or driving through a Chick-Fil-A, you get an understanding of what the culture is like. Faith-based, and efficient, every customer is treated with respect. More people are attracted to this brand and they are retaining customers. Look at where you are now, there is culture. How people express themselves politically, how they dress, and where they work. The organizations that you find yourself participating in have values. Some are clearly stated in the beginning, others go unsaid. Maybe you are living in a fairly religious city. The different sides of your town most likely determine your income level. There might be train tracks that separate the upper-middle class from the lower-income families. You were born into a culture. If you were born in the United States, then you are American. Then you are identified by the state you live in, then the county, and the city. You unconsciously become a product of your environment, whether it is superior or inadequate. This is something you had no control over when you were born. If you want to do something about your current situation, then you find out what it is that you lack. As you grow older it is important to learn more about your environment and how diverse it is. Core dimensions of diversity include age, race, ability, ethnicity, gender, and sexual orientation. The first step is accepting whatever the situation is. If you are the minority living close to the downtown area, why? If you live in the suburbs on the outskirts of the city, why? Were you bussed to school as a child? All of these dimensions are factors of how you think. I mentioned other parts of an individual at the start of this chapter for a reason. Do not think of this as a job application. I am not here to collect information to hire you. Your upbringing shaped the way you think about life today. The way you grew up has played a part in the creation of your personality. How you approach people. Whether you say "soda", "pop", or "coke" when describing a carbonated beverage. The way you emphasize certain syllables in words like caramel, tomato, data, or pecan. You are probably hearing the way your community pronounces these words. No matter what your living situation was you became conditioned to act a certain way because everyone else did. Most of the friends I had growing up came from single-parent households or had to live with different parents every week. This is something that I will never understand because I grew up with both parents. Does this make me better than them? Of course not. I have had friends that lived in terrible conditions in the past that are thriving now. My parents had the decision to send me to a school district that was predominantly white with little to no diversity or one with diversity. They sent me to schools that were just an extra ten minutes away. This was convenient because it was on the way to their jobs. Both of my parents are educators. As a black child, it was important to them that I would be exposed to different kinds of people. Ultimately, I am still close to some people from elementary through high school. I had plenty of friends that did not look like me. It did not matter what their ethnicity was, if we had common interests, then we respected each other. I was open to hearing their opinions on certain topics. This is how society grows in a positive direction. The world needs diversity. Without it, there is a lack of talent and new ideas. What do you do before you travel to a foreign location or a new place in general? You grab your phone or computer and look up the best places to eat or have fun. If you are traveling to a place with a national language different from yours, you learn how to communicate. When it comes to business deals overseas, you will not be successful unless you learn the language. If you do not understand then you can find a translator. How do you find one? Well, you must first build a relationship with someone who can speak the language and translate. You never know how valuable you might be to the person you are doing business with. Maybe you have something they need and they have something you want. All of this is great. Having connections to people in different countries is exciting. But none of this can be accomplished without knowing your cultural identity. What is it? Cultural identity is the sense of belonging you feel toward a group based on my earlier dimensions. Your nationality, race, ethnicity, gender, and religion. Once you figure these areas out, you figure out your self-perception. As you age you begin to root yourself in your values and morals. When you are younger, it is easier to change the way you think. This does not disqualify older people from changing their perspective, it just takes a bit longer. Change can be hard to accept. When you know yourself culturally, your level of self-awareness increases. In a situation where there is no wrong answer, you react according to your perspective. If you are in a diverse group, then you have the opportunity to see how person A reacts compared to person B. As you strengthen yourself mentally, it is important to see things from other sides. If you are stuck in your average ways that produce average results, then how are you going to grow? Yes, your cultural identity is important, you should not ignore that. But you cannot be surrounded by people that look like you for the rest of your life. This is where that fixed mindset comes from. The belief that you cannot be great at whatever you put your mind to. The idea is that people are "born with it" and do not work for it. The false belief that your religion, values, and race are superior. This is not a useful way to live. You do not have to fully understand someone from a different country. You did not live the exact way they did. Nowadays more companies are looking for talent everywhere. Maybe for sales reasons or the greater good of society. Either way, there is no limitation when it comes to diversity in the workplace. This is not about using people. To attract diverse candidates, they need to be inspired. What if they say someone that looked like them or someone from the same location that succeeded. Someone that came from roughly the same conditions triumphs. How does that make them feel? Motivated to do more for themselves and put their city on the map. A community grows from multiple voices from different areas. When these voices come together and agree on something, great things happen. For teams, there must be shared values that relate to a common goal. When I was in high school my head football coach introduced all of us to the concept of "6 Strong." This was a list of six words that our team was built on. The first was courage. The next four were commitment, consistency, character, and communication. The last one was, you guessed it, culture. Now, what do the other five have to do with you? Character; integrity. What you do when no one is watching and when no one is clapping for you is key. When you are alone you should pay attention to your thoughts. One side of you will say "you can eat those cookies. It's just one. No one will ever know." The other side is saying, "imagine what you can eat instead of those cookies. Maybe all you need is something sweet. Try this fruit." When you face temptation your character will either be strengthened or weakened. Sure you can skip a step in your diet and eat a few cookies. It will not kill you.

But if your goal was to avoid sweets and you did not, then you lost. When the teacher left the room for one minute, were you the one cracking jokes or finishing your work? When you made progress in your field without anybody around to congratulate you, were you still proud of yourself? This leads to commitment. If I am being honest I believe that most people have commitment issues. Myself included. Nobody likes to evaluate the way they are living, especially when they are comfortable. When you commit you are also signing next to the word consistency. Are you willing to wake up earlier to work out? Are you willing to stay late to finish? Remember, nobody is perfect. There will be days that are physically and mentally draining. Pushing through when it hurts can unlock a second wind. You are giving yourself a boost. The mind and body are being taught how to fight through the storm, whatever that looks like. You will fall. But you must get up. There is time to regroup and change your approach. During summer conditioning if someone was far behind the pack, we would go back on the field and help them finish. Communication can be verbal or nonverbal. When teams are well connected, they are unstoppable. The chemistry is there. Each player knows their role and how they help the team win. This seems to be the missing piece of the puzzle. Sometimes when we are on teams we leave the communication to the assumed leader. Involving others and asking for their input is a good practice. More members of the team will feel inclined to contribute. Teams have high standards. Leading by example or through words is something everyone can do. Sometimes we walk into an organization with many assumptions. We assume that there is one leader and everyone is under one voice. We assume that there are too many voices and no one leading. We assume that we are just another number in the store, the firm, or the department. How we feel about ourselves plays a big role in the way we operate in groups. If we lack respect for ourselves, then it is hard to respect others. Maybe the one thing holding you back can change the dynamics of the groups you are involved in. The one part of yourself that you are ignoring could impact millions. But you will never know if you continue to live in a bubble. This is why we need community. We build lasting relationships with others. Exploring different cultures will broaden your mind. You learn new techniques and norms from people that seem foreign to you. Your interests can be seen as skills. Throughout your life, you might have devoted time to getting better. Now that you are in a place with diversity, you start to believe. The belief is that you can accomplish anything by being consistent and working harder than most. This is what the growth mindset is. You do not have control of what happens to you throughout your day. You can control the way you react and evaluate. Everyone wants to get closer to their dreams, but few put in the work. Your brain will make excuses that are hard to disapprove of. In these moments, you must go back to your "why." It is all connected. Whatever drives you, whatever wakes you up in the morning, allows consistency. This builds your character. As you prepare for the next milestone you gain confidence. As you explore other cultures you gain awareness. The goal is to thrive. A committed individual acknowledges the obstacles and then finds a way. When you are driving and you see a ripped tire or tree branch on the road, you have to react. Depending on how fast you are going this means swerving left or right to avoid hitting the object. Hopefully, you have enough time to react, but oftentimes you do not. Whatever the object is, it seems like it popped up out of nowhere. You cannot stop because other drivers are around you. If you stop, the estimated time of you getting to the next destination is delayed. Imagine how slow the traffic would be if everyone stopped and focused on the barriers. More people would be okay with stopping or slowing down if it meant they were comfortable. They become paralyzed by the excuses they conjure. The barriers seem to grow exponentially to where the individual has no control. We must go about our daily life with a different mindset. Instead of stopping and being overwhelmed, one should recognize and move forward. One thing is certain, everyone will face resistance. When you walk into a gym, what do you see? People working alone, some might be with partners, and others might be in groups. Maybe you walked passed the yoga class to get to the machines. There is diversity. Some people appear overweight, others look like seasoned bodybuilders. This is a central location for those looking to gain or lose weight. For some, this is therapy. Running for a certain amount of time makes them feel good. Lifting weights makes them feel alive. The struggle to reach a personal record, the chase is the exciting part. The gym humbles you. The first thing you might like to do when you walk in is compare yourself to others. Which is unhealthy. The journey is different for every single person you see. What you have in common is location and loyalty to that gym. Yet each person carries a different story.

Everyone has different goals set for themselves. If you have been working out for a while, then you know how busy gyms get in January. The flood of newcomers; new people to connect with. The elderly are doing water aerobics, teens are benching and squatting, and moms and dads are on the machines and treadmills. Everyone is putting forth the effort to get better. Instead of sitting around at home, these people get out of the house and push themselves. This is the culture. This is a part of the population that seeks discomfort. It is not easy to choose a workout over a lazy day at home. Getting a quick workout while working full-time and taking care of children is not easy. Humbling yourself when you feel prideful can be a challenge. After a few months of working out, you realize that you are better than no one. Physically speaking, maybe you are stronger than most. But how does that help you grow? The muscle itself does not grow without being broken down first. The right fuel is essential too. Results are not instantly visible. One push-up is not going to give you the strength to bench three hundred pounds, but it is a start. When you are starting as a rookie in your field, you learn from others. When you associate with people further along than you, you add their strategies to your work. You start to emulate them, not in a copy-paste way. This is accomplished by using their original tactics and modifying them to fit your goals. Success for you might be owning a home one day and raising a family. It might be becoming the first 'fill in the blank' in your family. When you know yourself, you might be able to give your community something meaningful. Maybe you can change the narrative that people before you have believed their whole life. Everyone loves a comeback story, a story where the main character beats all odds. Today, you have the opportunity to beat all odds, fictional and real. Be that committed person. Be the one with great character and watch what happens. Great things come to those who work consistently. Communicate with new people; explore what is outside the norm for you. You might run into a future business partner, spouse, or lifelong friend. Have fellowship with others. No matter how far you want to go with your dreams, you will need assistance. Link with those ahead of you. You have decided to invest in yourself. The return on investment is unlimited if you continue. Believe in yourself.

CHAPTER 5

DELAYED GRATIFICATION

W hat is delayed gratification? I would say most of us are more familiar with instant gratification. When you order next day shipping on that item you "really" wanted. Maybe you ordered food and the delivery driver showed up earlier than you expected. When you posted that picture of yourself, you made sure you got the right angles so you can get as many likes as possible. You constantly refresh the app so you can see who likes it. As you drive around town at night, you see the places that are still open past midnight. Imagine your local donut shop is open at 1 o'clock and you want two cake donuts and some hot chocolate. The workers will instantly give you your donuts after the transaction. Delayed gratification is refusing to act on impulse for an instant reward in the hopes of gaining an even better reward in the future. It is abstaining from short-term pleasure for long-term results. The problem is that technology today has allowed people to receive anything they want quickly. Nobody wants to wait anymore. No one wants to work hard. They would rather get the pleasure now than later. Advertisements like "lose 10 pounds in 10 days" as well as others have been placed in front of us. If everyone else is doing it, then why stand out? Why would you want to practice this weird thing called "delayed gratification?" This is not a huge trend, but it has been picking up recently. Picture yourself, five years old. You are sitting at the kitchen table. Your mom walks in with your favorite cookie. She places it on a nice napkin. She tells you that if you wait exactly ten minutes, then the cookie is yours and you will get ice cream. However, if you do eat the cookie before the ten minutes is up, you forfeit the ice cream. Since the attention span of a five-year-old is not long, the easy way out is to eat the cookie. It is right in front of you. You can instantly get that warm feeling when you first bite into a fresh chocolate chip cookie. But if you want to delay the reward because you want the ice cream, then you will have to wait. Let's say you did wait and you received. Compare that to a time when you acted on impulse. Maybe you bought something expensive in a store and tried to flex on your friends. You do all of this for attention. Think about why you did it. Maybe your self-esteem was contingent on outside approval. To get in that friend group and not be an outcast, maybe you did buy those shoes, that makeup, or that accessory. This is seen in children from elementary through high school. Kids are racing to get their parents to buy the newest phone, newest shoes, newest whatever. Why? To look cool in front of their friends. Maybe to set the next trend. In an instant, they get what they want. If you have ever grown up around people who seem to get what they want all the time, it is unpleasant. They complain about their place in line. The item they ordered was supposed to come Tuesday and it did not arrive until Friday. They treat the waiter with disrespect because they asked for light ice and got a cup full of ice instead. But this is not about them. Whoever you thought of is probably the example that you would not follow. If you have children, you would keep your distance from this person. Again, think about this person, but look at yourself. Have you been participating in activities that overflow you with gratification? Some people are more impulsive than others. Some people have more control over it than others. We are all impulsive in some way. In its truest definition, an impulse is an urge to act. It is a strong urge. What I think about is impulsive shopping. Take the grocery store for example. If you have been around long enough, you know that it might not help you to shop in a grocery store while hungry. Say you planned to cook three meals per day for the week ahead. You walk into the store starving. The list you made yesterday was simple, eggs, chicken breast, lean ground beef, black beans, rice, broccoli, and a case of water. But since you are in a state of hunger that seems unbearable, you go off-script. The first aisle you go to is full of cereal. The oversaturation of each box of sugar catches your eye. The colors and the googly-eyed characters seem to reel you in. So you grab the Fruity Pebbles, Lucky Charms, and Cinnamon Toast Crunch. Now you have three boxes of cereal. You remember that you have not had a sandwich in a long time. The next thing you grab is some bread, then some lunch meat. You walk past the ground beef and chicken breast. There is even a deal on both of them, but you keep walking. Within a couple of minutes, you find yourself grabbing five frozen pizzas. Fast forward a few more minutes, and you are grabbing a couple of two liters and chocolate milk. By the end of your trip, the only item that you grabbed on your list was eggs. On your way home, you go through a drive-thru and get two cheeseburgers and a large serving of fries. Just a snack, right? By the time you get home, the groceries are in the refrigerator, you are throwing away the wrappers from the fast-food you scarfed down. You realize that you accomplished nothing on this shopping trip. You allowed yourself to be distracted and you grabbed items that give you temporary pleasure. They taste good, they are not healthy. The food you grabbed will not fuel your body well for the next workout. Cereal, sandwiches, pizza, and soda are not going to help you lose that weight. You remember the tags on the ground beef and chicken. There was a major deal that does not happen often for the food that you could have purchased to build muscle. At this moment, you are suffering from buyer's remorse. The feeling of regret washes over you like a tidal wave. Just three hours ago you were ready to eat healthier. At the time, it felt good to get what you wanted. But there are no signs of the reward you truly desire. This is an extreme example that might not happen as often as you think. Even so, you must stay focused on the potential long-term benefits. You can look at this as a process in small steps to big steps. A simple situation is this one. You want to eat healthier. How does this happen? First, you can track what you are already eating. Next, you could look up simple recipes that include more nutrients. If you are not exercising regularly, maybe you join a gym or start walking in the park. Then you make a list of items that will provide the proper nutrition you need daily. This is not complicated. Maybe the first step is eating a few more fruits and vegetables. Maybe it is replacing time binge-watching your favorite show with a light jog on a trail. It might feel like you are sacrificing something valuable, but that does not mean it goes away. Continuing on a path that yields no results knowingly, is not going to get you anywhere. We have all fallen into the trap of instant gratification. There is no fulfillment because we are always chasing the next feeling. We get lost in the new standard of living that we see on tv and our phones. So what is stopping people from delaying gratification? As mentioned before, social media seems to be at the forefront. We see how our favorite celebrities and influencers are living and we want that lifestyle. This is a place where people are rarely opening up about their problems. There is nothing wrong with that because privacy is important. The whole world does not need to know. But if you truly need help, then there is nothing wrong with asking for resources. The second reason why delaying gratification is a tough ask is friends. People you hang around when you are looking for a good time. This includes destructive activities when they go unchecked like clubbing, drinking, and smoking. Besides a night of short-term fun and a possible hangover, there is not anything valuable that you gain from these people. This specific group only meets to have fun and not talk business. This group loves to complain about the work week and count down the days to the weekend. They cannot wait to drink and forget about their responsibilities. All they do is consume. This brings me to the next point. Overconsumption. A simple word that covers so many parts of our lives. When you are constantly scrolling and scrolling, liking every picture you see, you are wasting time. When you binge-watch three seasons of a popular show in three days, you excessively consume. The world wants you to overeat, and chase pleasure because after all, you only have one life. You might as well have as much fun as you can before you die. Anyone who wants to succeed must know how to deal with the temptation to overindulge. When you keep participating in activities that waste time, it makes those activities boring. After a while, the spark just is not there. It is not fun anymore because it is done every day. Eating your favorite cake on your birthday once a year is enjoyable. But if you had that same cake for a whole year straight, it would lose its special taste. Soon it would taste bad or you would have to eat a sweeter, tastier piece of cake. Delayed gratification is important because it teaches discipline. The earlier you start, the easier it is to implement later on when you feel like you consumed too much. When you abstain from certain activities, it makes them feel even better; with moderation. An advantage of practicing this is the separation from the majority of people. Most people do not realize they are overconsuming until they lose money, are heartbroken, or get a bad diagnosis. I do not want you to be like everyone else. You should not want to be average. If you are feeling lost and have no idea where to start, then try replacing the consumption with creation. Replace those destructive habits with creativity. Create something. A new workout routine, a new meal, a piece of music. Do it for yourself. Seek no validation from those around you. See how you feel about the piece of work you created. You will feel more accomplished than someone sitting on the couch wishing. Spend some time thinking about some new habits to adopt, evaluate, then install. When you spend some time away from social media and your so-called friends, you learn a few things about yourself. The truth is, you do not desperately need social media to survive. The people you hang out with on weekends are not going anywhere. Meaning, you do not have to see them every day. If you are young, then you will go your separate way eventually. Do not be afraid of that. If you are a bit older, then maybe you need to weigh the pros and cons of associating with these people. When you work on your purpose and learn new skills you gain experience. Think of this as a video game. The life you have is the only one you get. So it is only right to do everything in your power to become the best version of yourself. The more skills you have at your disposal, the more valuable you become. Then you match the skills you have gained with your purpose. Suddenly you are a machine; it feels like no one can stop you from winning. When you lose, you learn. You do not dwell in the past like those around you. The losses are lessons and the wins are blessings. You get to a certain point, you are not at the top. The mentality is continuous improvement. Even if you are at the "top" you try your hardest to stay there. At this point, you are living your dream. The picture-perfect life you show others on social media is real. The people that are looking to improve ask you how you did it. While there are several actions you took along the way, one part that stands out is delayed gratification. When you kept winning and the urges were high to celebrate and spend money on yourself, you stayed disciplined. Every win was simply another stair-step as you kept going up. This little, overlooked practice is extremely important. Do not let the fear of being judged take over. In reality, you will be judged either way. If you choose your purpose over the pleasure, then your group will miss. All of a sudden you are 'too good for them, and you fail to waste time with them. Opinions from these people no longer hold you down. You are not seeking advice from those that are slowly destroying themselves. The truth is, there is envy due to the lack of progress in their own lives. They see you as one of them. They see your success and how happy it is making you. Yet they are still in the same place financially, mentally, and physically. The jealousy grows because they do the bare minimum and expect the same results as you. They believe in balance. Unfortunately, their idea of balance is working five days a week and partying through the other two days. You are on a different path. As soon as you realized you needed to change, you took the steps. On the other hand, when they knew they needed to change, they kept doing the same things. Why? They were afraid of separating. Each time they consumed they attached their identity to the good times. Scrolling endlessly, eating junk food, not exercising, not creating something. All of these habits caused this person or that group to feel a lack of purpose. A lack of purpose leads to wasted potential. While potential does not guarantee success, the active pursuit will produce some results at the least. As long as you are actively going after your goals, you will accomplish something. Chasing instant gratification will hold you back. Whether you like it or not, you will become conditioned to go to these sources of pleasure. In addition to this, the feeling does not last long. You cannot stoop to the level of those who lack ambition. Remove yourself from anything that does not serve you. By serve, I do not mean people that support every little thing you do. Everybody needs accountability. You deserve to be around people that call you out when you are wrong. Instant gratification gives us a false sense of accomplishment. Our lives feel complete when we finally finish our favorite tv shows. The workweek was stressful so the only way to solve that was to drink and party. If you could forget about how bad your week was, you will not have to worry about your obligations. Right? Procrastination is a result of instant gratification. We are living at a point in time where procrastination is easier than ever. Our technology is within an arm's reach every hour of every day. Social media is not something that has been around for a century. It may be fairly old to some while others have grown up with it. Decades ago, these distractions did not exist. Schools have gone from chalkboards to projectors to smart boards to virtual meetings. This speeds up the process of teaching.

Now the debate on which is better for the student is dependent on the student. You cannot place everybody under the same category, as we all learn differently. Procrastination is delaying something when you know the result of delaying it is negative. What about gratification? If you deserve to feel happy then why do you have to delay it? There is a difference. Remember a time when you procrastinated and it did not work out. More often than not you are not maxing out your time to execute the work given to you. The classic scenario is this. Jimmy is in the seventh grade, he has a final project where he has to invent something or upgrade an established invention. It is February. The rubric that his teacher gave him says the project is due on the first Friday of May. The project is worth two hundred points. Jimmy has a high C in the class. Not bad. Not above average. Jimmy is addicted to video games. His parents forced him to play sports but he never enjoyed it. He does not participate in any clubs or organizations. When he gets home he throws his bag down and plays video games. He only comes out of his room when it is time to eat. When he does get homework done, it is usually after midnight. His sleep schedule is off. Each day in class, he is in and out of sleep. Throughout the semester, he continues this cycle. He began this school year with a good GPA, now his grades are slipping. He treats every class like this. A few weeks pass by, nothing has been done. But he has some time. A couple of months go by. It is April now. Not much time left, but he can still turn in something. Now he is one week out from the due date. Finally, Jimmy started on this project. He is racing to get this project done. Every hour he spent on video games is now dedicated to finishing. If he had this same intensity, in the beginning, he would not have to worry about his grade. By this time, he would have been preparing to present. Consequently, he is rushing everything. He puts together an invention that is out of order. Jimmy does not know what it is, he is building something irregular, gluing and taping. There is no time to think. Since he chose short-term pleasures, he sacrificed long-term success. He sacrificed his grade to play video games. By the first Friday of May, all he has is a shoebox with paper towel rolls taped to it. He called it a super toaster. All of his classmates have amazing inventions. Everyone else turned in quality work. Jimmy can tell that they paid attention to the rubric. They went above and beyond for the two hundred points. Now he feels ashamed of himself. One thing is certain, he cannot get the time back.

It is the end of the year and there is nothing he can do to change his C to a B. Is this about grades? No. Jimmy's procrastination caught up to him. He thought he had time. He believed that he could put off the work until he felt like it. If we are being honest, we have all been in similar situations. We had the option to choose growth in the future over temporary joy. Maybe you ignored the work that had to be done. There is nothing you can do about it now. If you learned your lesson, then you will be prepared for the next time you feel like procrastinating. To truly grow you must take ownership. Jimmy could do all the work to never make the mistake again, but if he does not admit to his mistakes, then he will continue to procrastinate. The cycle needs to be broken. Throughout middle and high school, chasing that instant happiness was normal. Everyone was focused on what everyone else was doing. Some people based their lives on others that were not doing any better. The one with the newest whatever had the popularity. If you came from money, you would be at the top. If you did not come from money, then you were left in the dust. Many people were not being their true selves. The talent and skills that they had were suppressed because they were concerned about how others would feel. When you scroll on social media, your mind is wandering. You look at everyone else's lives and feel empty. One can argue that there needs to be a balance between work and life. Balance is an even distribution. The hardest workers in history, your favorite players, actors, actresses, and musicians did not have balance. Maybe some did, but most did not. Why? They were on their purpose and had to put in the extra work. If you are trying to be the best at what you do and you are doing the same things that the majority are doing, then you will not be better. I do not believe balance is a fictional idea. But if you want to come close to your greatest self, you are going to have to do more. In some cases, you might be on your own. If your workout partner is not there to push you through, then what are you going to do? This goes back to integrity. Balance is what you think it is. If going to the club every weekend with your friends feels like balance, then keep going. Nobody is stopping you. But look at yourself. Be completely real with yourself. If you were in the best shape financially, physically, and mentally; would you be searching for help? To be fair, just because you are in a great position in life does not mean you should not keep learning. While this is true, the individuals that want to make a change put in the work. Months later, years later you see their progress and it is surprising. The people around them did not expect them to make it, that is why they are surprised. When you witness these people hit rock bottom and upgrade themselves, the stories are inspiring. Check-in with yourself. Why would you wait to hit rock bottom? Why would you wait until a family member dies, or you go through a near-death experience to change? Do not be overwhelmed by these questions, but please consider them. Soon the procrastination will catch up to you. Time is something you cannot get back, and when it is wasted it feels even worse. Delayed gratification will help you appreciate all the activities that made you happy. Now you have structure. You have something to look forward to. People who have nothing to look forward to, drag through the week. They complain without making an effort. There will be days when you are just grinding. Sometimes you will have to put your head down and execute. There is nothing wrong with that. Think of something you can look forward to. While you wait, work. Keep hitting those milestones to get in the best position you can. When you prepare, you will not need to leave anything on the table. Each day is another opportunity to succeed. Receiving everything you want in an instant will hinder your growth. Sometimes you have to wait and trust the process. Sometimes you will not hit that personal record before going through what feels like hell first. Instant gratification will rob you of time. You must do what is in front of you. Delayed gratification is not delayed happiness. You deserve to be happy in the process just as much as when you get the result you wanted. This takes practice. A little each day goes a long way. Try it.

Take a couple of hours or a couple of days off from the things that bring you that temporary feeling.

CHAPTER 6

HATERS VS SUPPORTERS

S o you want to be great? You want to become the best version of yourself. Fantastic! You have practiced. You are one of the few that are taking steps; sacrificing. For some time you have felt separated from the crowd in a good way. The transition from static to dynamic is in full effect. But there are two types of people that have not left your side. Haters and supporters. They could be close, within your family, or behind a screen. Maybe you know them well, maybe you have no idea who they are. Usually, when you decide against the norm, or outside the expectations, you receive some backlash. You get bombarded with questions. Why do these people care about the moves you are making? Why are they so focused on you? The voices never stop. Everyone shares what is on their mind. They are critics, self-proclaimed experts. Haters dislike your process. They see you get better each day while they stay miserable. If you grew up in the same area, then there is a possibility for even more animosity. How could you be successful when you came from such humble beginnings? Right? Their excuses hold no weight, yet their presence is heavy. There are some strategies that you can use when dealing with people on both sides of the spectrum. The question you are probably asking yourself is, "how can I deal with haters and supporters?" One thing is certain, no matter where you go there will always be people praising or questioning what you do. This is the reality that you must accept to move forward. If you have not already grasped this concept before, then recognize that you need distance. These people are near you all the time. This should not grant them full access to you and your time. After all, your time and energy should be spent on your purpose. As hard as it is, stepping away from certain people takes practice. Continuing on the same path will give you the same results. By now you should have an idea of what you want out of life. Your environment should help you, not hurt you. So you need to create separation from the people that do not support you. You create distance by sticking to a solid routine and getting to work. Make the conscious effort to go through the pain of discipline by yourself. With a tight circle, there will only be a select few that you share your wins with. These are your supporters. Haters and supporters can equally damage your growth or build it. Envy is something that shows up at an early age. In elementary, there was probably an individual that had all the friends and popularity. This person was the one with a group of people around them at recess. Maybe this person was always asking questions and finishing first on big tests. You envied them because they had all the qualities and so-called "luck" in their life. The same pattern repeated in high school. There is a possibility that you focused more on what others had than what you had. After all, it is easier to compare yourself to everyone because of the connectivity we have today. You can look at success with envy or with admiration. Let's say you take the envy route. Now you have some built-up anger inside you because you lack what this person has. You want every ounce of success that they receive. The cars, mansion, purse, friends, all of it. Yet, the list of differences between you and this person is growing. Pretend this is a game. What you are viewing now is a level one-hundred player. You knew this person when you were both at level ten. They grew ten times bigger, while you did nothing. This is not to say that you have not been putting in the work. Maybe you have been grinding and nothing seems to click. You are aiming horizontally and not vertically. Since you chose envy, you are not changing anything. Your routine is inconsistent; your diet is inconsistent. Each day you wake up exhausted, mad at the world. It seems like everywhere you look someone else is winning while you are losing. You know deep down the work that needs to be done, but you keep dragging on. The work is ignored. From an outside eye, you have no drive. The days are wasted on instant gratification. Life is not looking good. You constantly project your insecurities. Every move someone makes you critique. Initially, you felt good when you questioned what they were doing. But not you are downcast. The friends you had, in the beginning, do not like hanging out with you because of your judgemental ways. Hating is a loose term. Criticism can be constructive and destructive. When it is constructive someone is telling you that you are not reaching your full potential. You are being built up. The destructive criticism is meant to tear you down. When you receive criticism, you have two options. The first option is using the words as fuel to push you. The second option is often involuntary. Criticism might always look destructive to you because your ego blocks the real message. So when you do receive this, you are paralyzed. You do not know how to react because their opinions are meaningful to you. Choosing whether or not to value their opinion is completely up to you. You have that freedom to sort these voices into valuable or useless. If you are putting in the work and seeing the results, pretty soon you will gain some haters. Notice how I did not say, followers. You gain haters. Like I said in the beginning, these people might be close to you. They might be people you least expected. The fact is they are watching every step you take; with envy. When you announce the launch of your business, there they are commenting "it will never work" and "you will not make money from this." Luckily, you chose to take a risk. You might be growing faster than them. The purpose you have sought out is at the top of your priority list. The haters do not understand. They have no idea what you are doing when no one is watching. Instead of spending time on mindless activities, you went a different way, and they are intimidated by your power. To avoid some of the hate, you can take a break from social media and all other forms of contact with these people. Take a month off from social media and see what it does. I would not be sharing this with you if it did not work well for me. A month away or even a couple of weeks from social media will help you. The first benefit is that time you spend scrolling can be used for actual work. Another benefit is you will have nobody to compare yourself to but the person you were yesterday. When you are scrolling and liking posts, you are attracted to content that fits the life you want to live. You see an individual doing better than you and there is more envy than admiration. On the flip side of this, if you do choose to take a small break, you can learn how to look at successful people with admiration. You can even contact them and ask how they did it, and what challenges they faced along the way. With the extra time, you can study. It is okay to be a beginner and ask for assistance. Do not let your pride get in the way of you excelling. Social media is not the biggest problem, but it can be excessive when used improperly. When you take a break, you are working. The wins and losses you accumulate do not have to be posted or shared with anyone. You are by yourself celebrating the small wins and learning. When you come back some people will say you went on a hiatus. This is true. You paused the time you spent trying to impress them to reach your goals. Now when you come back and start to share what you have created, they will call you an overnight success. Little do they know the work you put in. The best part about that is, that they never need to know. It is up to you to open up. In your absence, they formed their opinions. They say things like "you changed" and "how come we never talk" well, you have been busy. Not the fake type of busy, but the authentic pursuit. By staying true to yourself, you looked fake to them. This is okay. You are not meant to stay the same. Haters might break you down but you must channel your feelings into energy to win. The journey will be tough. If you are in the middle of it right now, then you understand. But this is what you signed up for. In my experience, haters are essential. Why? When someone is doubting you, especially if they are close, it drives you crazy. With enough control and planning, you can turn that crazy into consistency. The consistency then turns into success. It is no longer about proving them wrong. You are testing yourself. There is a daily evaluation and the hate makes you want to win even more. Now that haters are out of the way, the spotlight is on supporters. People in your life that are fairly agreeable. Anything you say to them, they give their input with your best interest at heart. They want the best for you and enjoy seeing you take off. You share with them what you want to do in the future and they push you. Around these people, you are battling your ego and reality. Your ego will tell you that you already made it. When you share what you want to accomplish, at that moment it feels like it already happened. They congratulate you for sharing. The reality is, that you are not there yet. You are blinded by the good feeling you get around them. If you feel like you are already there, then it makes no sense to put in the work. This can cost you. Realize that supporters are not always reliable. Sure they might claim to be loyal, but some do not believe in you. They might be surprised by your progress, so they continue to validate you. I like to separate supporters into two groups, fighters, and flyers. Similar to fight-or-flight, these people respond based on their actions. In simple terms, you are the perceived threat. What you are doing is not ordinary. This can create stress and it might scare them away. You are in a fistfight with life and it is important to keep your hands up to protect your vision. Like any boxing match or UFC card, someone will get hit in the face. When you watch boxing live, in between rounds the cameras go to each corner. The microphone is on so you can hear what the boxer's coaches are saying. If you pay attention you can hear the critiques along with the motivation. These people tell the boxer to stay calm. There is also someone there to fix any cuts on the face. These are your fighters. They are there for you when you are winning. More importantly, they are there when you are losing. If they have been in a similar situation, they will offer some advice. At the same time, they will let you figure it out. This is the supporter you want. Maybe you have been a fighter for someone. When you watch them win, it is an amazing feeling. The relationship is mutual. What you have gained is what you give in return. The other side of this is the flyers. Flyers are like the passengers in your car that are just along for the ride. At the end of the day, you will get from point a to point b regardless of their input. They tend to only provide help when asked. Flyers may or may not check up on you. Sometimes they will not check on you unless you are winning. If it is popular to support you, they will. One positive quality is that flyers stay out of the way. They are not as active as fighters. When you are in a season of losing, they are nowhere to be found. This can leave you questioning their loyalty. The truth is you need both. If you want to be left alone most of the time, then it would be favorable to have more flyers in your life. If you need a support system that you can call upon at any time, then you would benefit from more fighters. When you have a fair amount of supporters, you feel powerful. Keep in mind the effects of success. If you let the success go to your head, then you will not feel like improving. As long as it feels real, it is real. Your supporters might stick around to hopefully be rewarded. There is some entitlement to the fruits of your labor. Although supporters are supposed to be there at all times, that might not be the case. It is still possible to support from a distance, just like it is possible to hate. An unhealthy way of coping would be to stop production. The haters can make you feel worthless. You might convince yourself that you are not worthy of winning. After years of losing, the winning might be overwhelming, causing you to slow down. As a result, you plateau or quit altogether. Too many supporters will grow your complacency. You will begin to be satisfied with how far you have come. The classic phrase "you did not come this far, to come this far" still rings true. To think that you have done enough is foolish. You can always get better. What people tell you should not dictate how you feel about your dreams. They are two sides of the same coin. When you get to your version of the top, they can easily switch sides. This is a part of the process. These people will come into your life and leave. It is not your job to keep track of every person. They are not doing the diet with you, they are not avoiding instant gratification with you. You are alone on this journey. If you want to feel less alone, then you can turn to your supporters and other people who invest in you. So now you have investors. They are not fighters or flyers. Investors give you what they can, then sit back and watch. Resources like funds and connections can put you in a higher place faster than most. Similar to building your community, mentors can help you network. Maybe you do not need a mentor right now. I have had mentors from different areas of my life that have impacted me. This can be a pastor, coach, friend, or family member. The key is to find someone that has already been through what you are facing right now. If they are thriving in their area of expertise, even better. Most of the mentors I had, I did not realize how much better they made me as a person. They devoted their time to help me win. These were high-character individuals that were always in my corner no matter what I did. My mentors were brave enough to check me if I was doing something wrong. They were able to show me the right way too. When I am looking for someone to trust, I want them to believe in themselves as well. If I cannot be told the truth, then everything is sugar-coated. I like the hard truth. When you receive it, it hurts. But it is for your good. The last thing you need to do is hang around a person that will not give you the facts. You cannot water down your work ethic to reach those goals that have been nagging at you. Too much of this will have you spinning your wheels wondering where to go next. An exceptional mentor will show you how they did and apply it to your situation. Anybody who has ever invested in anything is looking to get some return on investment. While these people are not completely responsible for your success, they still hold a special place on your journey. They are hard to forget. This is about making yourself proud while showing them that they made the right decision to move you closer. Depending on their connections, you might receive a once-in-a-lifetime opportunity. It is normal to be fearful and anxious. This is unknown. You cannot predict when you take off, but you can certainly control what you do in the meantime. Mentors take some of the weight off. When you receive opportunities, do not let them go to waste. There is a pain in losing, joy in winning and suffering in regret. Losing will teach you lessons and expose your weaknesses. Winning puts a spotlight on your strengths. Regret is the feeling you get when you know you could have done better, but you decided to hold back. It is a wave of sadness due to missed opportunities. When it happens, there is nothing you can do to change it. This is a reaction to the progress you have made thus far. It can last minutes, months, or even years. I do not want you to live with regrets. Nobody wants to be in a dark place mentally. Giving it your all and still losing is better than not trying. You failed, but at least you did not back down from the fight. Maybe you are accumulating tons of losses at this moment. But it will make your success story even sweeter. To come from impossible circumstances and still be standing today would be your testimony. Hopefully, the mentors in your life have testimonies. If it is something you can relate to, it makes you want to take action. Whether you like it or not, the clock is going to keep ticking. The sun will still rise in the east and set in the west. Your haters will still be present no matter where you go. The supporters might keep their distance as you continue to grow. The negativity can weaken you while the positivity wakes you up. Voices from the haters have the power to make you quit or rise to the occasion. The voices from the supporters can fill your head up and keep you motionless. I am challenging you to identify these people. This should not be a tough task because they show their true colors when they come in contact with you. Maybe you are not aware of this because they are your friends and family. Ask yourself who is actually in your corner. Who are the fighters? Who are the flyers? Is anyone investing in you today? I want this to be as simple as possible for you. If you are serious about your dreams and aspirations then you will consider both sides. To be extraordinary, you have to do extraordinary things. Easier said than done, but you get the point. Try not to shy away from these people. Appreciate the fact that they are in your life, some longer than others. If no one is hating on you, then you are simply not going hard enough. I know that is a tough pill to swallow. I was told the same phrase. We like to be right. We like to prove people wrong and say, "See! Look what I did!" and "You never believed in me. So I did it anyway." We like to put our success on display in the societal trophy case. When we lose, we do not like to share. When we win, everything seems to fall in place. Most people will let every voice change them for the worse. Some people thrive off of the validation of others. I want you to know that validation is not going to benefit you in the long run. If you are always seeking approval, when someone disagrees with your vision, you will fall apart. Feed off your validation. Create the energy from within. You know what you want. There is not a better time than now to act. When you start to work on your purpose, the people you need will reveal themselves. You might need to seek a mentor, but you can also attract one. People will want to hear your story. They are attracted to those that do the hard work when no one is watching. The ones that do not need to post every move they make are usually winning. Letting the world know what you are doing throws you off. It is optional, but so many people do it because they need that ego boost. They would rather look like they are winning instead of attacking the work. On the days that you are alone, chipping away, you will cherish the wins. Each win will feel like another step on the staircase. Of course, you will acknowledge them by yourself. Since you are not where you want to be yet, the temptation to share is lower. Most of the time, you will feel like you do not need to explain yourself. Soon their opinions will not matter. Take action now, do not wait.

CHAPTER 7

ADDICTION

We are all addicted to something. Technology makes almost anything and everything accessible. The world is upgrading everything to make life as comfortable as possible. Some of these activities are free in the sense of money. But it eats away at your time. It costs you potential gains in the future. Dopamine plays a part in the reward system. When you eat a piece of chocolate or play your favorite song, there is a rush of happiness. We naturally go back to what is familiar, and if the familiar is pleasurable, then we are hooked. I am guilty of this. You are guilty of this. No one is exempt. The most common addictions are nicotine, alcohol, marijuana, painkillers, and hard drugs. Some of the addictions that are talked about but ignored are social media, pornography, and isolation. In moderation, social media can be used to grow your business. At weddings and various celebrations, alcohol is served. If you have a headache or are recovering from an injury, painkillers reduce the horrible feelings. Even so, too much of these and you will be taking a step back in life. Overstimulation of what feels good at the moment will make every other moment minuscule. You will not enjoy the things you once had fun doing. The activities will feel like chores and you will start to feel burnt out. This is can lead to depression. The fire you once had was put out, stolen. The plants that you laid down the seeds for, killed. Finally, the person you see in the mirror is destroyed. Or so it appears that way. This is not a life sentence. You can break free from the chains both self-inflicted and forced. First, the main causes of addiction need to be identified. Addiction can stem from peer pressure, family history, and poor mental health. Peer pressure can be insurmountable. It is a force. In its full form, it can change your life forever. One bad decision can alter your trajectory. Forget about the cheesy commercials that point out the obvious. The resources are out there. All the information in the world cannot help you if you fail to apply it and take action. I have seen the effects of addiction due to peer pressure. A person on their way to success is derailed by drugs and alcohol. All it took was one time, and they fell down the slippery slope. When you lose a loved one or someone you grew up around, it hurts even more. The feeling of hopelessness starts to build. You start to wonder what you could have done. You blamed yourself for not seeing the signs. If the signs were clear, then you blamed yourself for not doing anything about it. In group settings, anybody can be a target. Usually, those with less experience with drugs and alcohol are targeted first. If they have no experience at all, then the likelihood of being under pressure increases. This is not a great position to be in. If you get pressured to do something every time you are out with your friends, then you need to evaluate your circle. Yes, you can have fun but that does not mean contorting yourself to fit the frame they want you to be in. You are not them and they are not you. With that being said, there are a few things you can do to avoid this. I assume that the reason why you keep getting singled out is that you are passive. You are the doormat. People take your kindness as weakness and abuse it. One thing you can do is start saying no to plans. If your friends are always going out every weekend, what are they accomplishing? If their dreams were to become alcoholics and drug addicts, then they would not feel miserable. But there it is, the contradiction. The usage of both might make them feel like they are at the top of the mountain, but the valley creeps up. A valley is an unpleasant place with hangovers, withdrawals, and more horrific obstacles. When the usage is not giving you enough pleasure, then you will search for something stronger. Now you are stuck in a cycle. It might start as monthly, then weekly. Soon it will become habitual. The craving will be there every day. If you are currently living in an environment where drug addicts and alcoholics are the majority, you are not alone. Many successful individuals today have come from rough areas. But at this moment, you are the focus. I want you to sit down with yourself for a few minutes. Think about what you are addicted to. The places, people, and activities; all of it. On the rainy days, who and what do you turn to? When you are in pain, how do you cope? If you are not comfortable with writing these down, then you can contemplate them. Becoming more self-aware of how you deal with the ups and downs can help you on your journey. Tapping into your feelings will allow you to take charge in a group setting when the pressure is on. Also, this will allow you to demand respect. Those people need to know that you are not the same person anymore. They might see you as the person you were in the past that was always there. Now that you created distance, you need to move accordingly. To illustrate, there was a time when I had to separate myself. I would tell you that all you have to do is ignore them, but that does not always work. In high school, I had plenty of close friends. Some inspired me and some that were not the best examples. I say this from a humble perspective because nobody is perfect. Most of my friends back then did not have both parents in one house. I understand that their upbringing is a factor when considering their behavior. This does not exclude those with both parents. Unfortunately, some of the people I spent time with came to school high and partied every weekend. Years ago I would have never thought some of them would go down the wrong path. Even some people I knew in elementary, the nicest, most respectful kids, turned addicts. People I believed in, people I loved; wasting their lives on the chase of instant pleasure. Some people engage in these activities to look cool. They do not want to be thrown out of the group. Fitting in is more important to them than being authentic. I want you to be your true self. If that means that you have to leave that friend group that does not serve you, so be it. Too many people are afraid of this. It is normal. Detaching from the comfortable is a hard task, but once you do it the rewards are sweeter. In the end, you never desperately needed these people. Consequently, you will still have a love for them and wish them the best. A part of you might want to pull them along, even if they are dead weight. Keep in mind how that might limit your progress. I separated myself when I found out that the friend group cared more about how many people they could sleep with. On top of that, they loved to vape and drink. They would find an excuse to party every weekend. In these crucial years of learning, they decided to go another way. I would be lying if I said I never participated. Once I followed them, I quickly felt the need to leave. My time was valuable. I was focused more on the future. After hanging out with them a few times, I started to feel lazy. My only desire was to have fun. While you are young, this is not the worst thing you can do. But some of them started getting into some tough situations. Being arrested, sharing sexual content, and selling drugs. Thankfully, none of them are in jail, but a few came close. I share this because I could have been in the same position if I did not check myself. They gave me examples of what not to do. So I tried to apply what I learned daily. Look back on your past addictions, then look at your current addictions. Understand that you are not your past. You do not live there anymore. A weak mindset can paralyze you and leave you questioning your self-worth. Maybe you had supportive friends that kept you on the right track. In contrast, your family history might be the stronger cause. One thing you cannot change is your genetics. You do not get to pick what family you are born into. For instance, a family full of alcoholics. It all started with two people. You know how reproduction works, so I will save that. If one person started drinking and their children were exposed to that at an early age, the trend kept going. What seems like an endless loop of alcoholics following in the footsteps of their mothers and fathers. So where do you fit in? As of right now, you are still alive and will hopefully raise a family one day. Some people vow to never be like their parents. Especially if they lost their lives due to addiction. The families that deal with addiction and poverty usually have one member that changes everything. You can be the first. If someone has already accomplished this, then you can be the next. You have the opportunity to break generational curses. Wealthy families did not become wealthy by accident. Someone said, "I will be the one." Maybe not in those exact words, but something like it. You have two choices. The easy route brings the most pleasure in the short term but there is a pain in the future. The harder route will require time, energy, and sometimes tears. Being disciplined will be painful at times. You are trading pain now for delight in the future. This road is narrow, it has one lane. The easy road is wide with thousands of lanes. It is not too late to take the exit. Decision after decision. You might feel trapped, after all, if it is in your family history, it feels unavoidable. But you do not deserve to check yourself in the box of alcoholism, substance abuse, disease, or anything else that runs in the family. If you are struggling, one way to attack it is by identifying triggers. A trigger is something that brings up powerful emotions that make you desire drugs or alcohol. This could be a certain smell, place, or maybe a person. Make that trigger known. If you have tried to quit in the past, then you already know what it is. It might be a list. Now that you have identified them, the next time you get triggered, you will have a plan. When the emotions are high and you experience this, take mental note of how you feel. Think about what got you to this mental space. Both the good and bad. Retrace your steps. Define whether or not this was intentional or unintentional. An intentional situation would mean that you knew what would happen, but you felt like willpower could keep you level-headed. On the other hand, an unintentional situation would mean that you had little control over the circumstances. To some degree, you do have control over some circumstances. If your environment is not one of them, then I advise you to stay vigilant. Your life is valuable even if you do not believe it. When triggers strike, you either relapse or get stronger. This does not have to be a complicated process. The more bells and whistles you have in this part of your life, the more stress will accumulate, and you will not believe in yourself as a result. This is where you can turn your situation into a game. The game is you against the person you were yesterday. You are competing with no one else but yourself. You are your toughest opponent. Being stuck in your ways can and will defeat you. It might not be in an instant, it could be gradual. Play the game. Start by changing one part of your routine. Take small steps if you need to. This cannot happen overnight. You cannot eliminate all the triggers, but if you know how to deal with them, you will be further than most. Similar to an addiction gradually making you worse, you can gradually make yourself better. Start small. If you have been doing this for years, then it is going to take more than one week to leave the faulty habits. Decrease your consumption. Instead of smoking three cigarettes a day, try two, then one. No matter what the number is, lower it by one or two each time. Cigarettes are just one example. With new devices like vapes and electronic cigarettes, more people have access to them. I have seen people fiend over one hit of nicotine while denying their addiction. There was a point in time when they tried it once. Maybe their circle was full of smokers so they did not want to feel left out. When you try the method of slowly decreasing your consumption, you will get used to using less. The feeling of needing more might stay with you for a bit but it will be worth it. Before I think about reverting to old habits, I like to picture two people in my head. The first person I visualize is the person I was before I started this addiction. What would that version of me think of me now? If my past self could watch my current self, would they be proud? The answer might not be what you want, but it is what you need. The second person I visualize is my future self. If I continue down this path what will the future me look like? Alternatively, if I change my path, will the future me thank the current me for sacrificing? While no technology will allow you to talk to yourself in the past, or get a sneak peek of the future; you can still do something about it. What you do today directly affects tomorrow and so on. Do this for yourself. You are the only person you can fully control. It is you that lives with you each day. Waking up in regret is not something I want for you. Your addictions strip away your confidence. It is like you are walking around with a bear trap around your ankle. The bear trap is only visible to you and not to the outside world. You walk around limping, and no one knows what is wrong with you. The strength needed to get out of the trap is in you. But you have not taken the steps to unlock it. When you try to chase your goals, your feet start to hurt. There is no way that you can catch up. So you think. It could be one trap, or two. This weight that has been slowing you down for months or years on end needs to be taken off immediately. You should not associate yourself with the person you were in the past. As you work to beat the addiction that harms you, the traps start to loosen. The springs compress and soon the traps will be open. What you do after is important. Another cause that can stem from family history and peer pressure is poor mental health. Mental health is a topic that is often swept under the rug. At a young age, maybe you had to mature faster than others. Especially if you experienced a traumatic event early on. If you put nothing else first in your life, your emotional well-being should be in the top two on your list of priorities. The relationships you build, the finish lines you cross, and the actions you take all start in the mind. The way you process the loss of a family member or the birth of a child. When you are facing a giant in the middle of the storm, where is your head at? There is no destination called perfect mental health. For some, it is a battle every waking hour. For others, it is a simple task in the structure of each month. I want you to have a solid foundation. One that will not be destroyed when you face the high winds and storms of life. What I have gone back to for the past few years is exercise. Physical activities like walking, jogging, swimming, and dancing can lower feelings of anxiety and depression. If you enjoy other ways to express yourself you could make art, read books, start a garden, cook; the list goes on. Hobbies that include meeting new people can help improve your communication skills. If your friends are involved, that is okay too. Make sure that you are around the positive ones. You should not have to edit your personality to fit in. The results of doing that for too long will only produce anxiety and depression. Juggling different versions of yourself that are not the real you, will make you unfulfilled and exhausted. But you will be fulfilled. What you want is something meaningful to come from this life of yours. As much as it helps to be mindful and seek assistance internally, you must look outside yourself. Willpower is not enough. You must seek external help. This will not be found in the same environment where you picked up on this addiction. There is someone out there who is near you that has been through practically the same thing. If you cannot reach a person like this then you can seek therapy from various apps and centers available to you. Now if those options do not work for you at all, then you can evolve by shifting your energy. This is not some guru method that has been studied for centuries. It is transmutation. To one that does not know what the word means, it might sound like a fatal chemical reaction that turns a scientist into a monster in a sci-fi movie. I assure you it is not. But you will see some drastic changes if you fully commit. Transmutation is the act of transitioning from one nature or behavior to another. This is when you transfer the energy used to engage in your addiction into other activities with benefits. When you transmute, it is similar to the strategy I previously explained. The only exception is you do not consume less of what is holding you back, you make the effort to replace it. For example, someone who sits and streams their favorite movies for two hours every weekend can replace that time. On Saturdays, they can take a walk outside for an hour and then research some easy, healthy meals to cook. This will prepare them for the rest of the weekend. On Sundays, they can cook meals and watch some videos related to cardio. Even though watching movies takes little energy, it is not benefitting the health of the viewer. This can snowball into other problems, like overeating and drinking too much. The result could be obesity and a higher risk of some cancers. Granted these are merely predictions of what this lifestyle can do to the body when left unchecked. Transmutation shifts your focus and rewrites your thought process. All addictions start with a thought, then an urge, and finally the action. So if you can change the way you think, then you can beat addiction. This is why it is important to identify your triggers early so that you can be ready. The urges might not ever go away. But it is up to you to get out of your head. Transmutation will help guide your thoughts along paths that lead to a healthier lifestyle. The activities you replace your addiction with will not be exciting when you start. At first, it will be ugly; unattractive. With consistency, you will find that they become enjoyable. No one has to join you if you do not want them to. These are your hobbies and interests that you can devote more time to. They do not necessarily take your mind off what you overcame. However, you could still be stuck in your addiction. It is a reminder to try new things and have some variety in your life. Life can feel dull when you engage in the same mindless behaviors. Maybe you can find your purpose while overcoming addiction. You have the potential to educate others and share your strategies. On your journey through recovery, having at least one person you can rely on can be the key to success. This is not mandatory. I grew up in the church. I built a relationship with four other people. I grew up around them, seeing them at least once a week for nearly eight consecutive years. They are my brothers that I never knew I needed. As we grew older, we spent time doing stupid things in public, but we also had meaningful conversations. I could tell them anything, and they could tell me anything. In dark times, we kept each other motivated. Time would go by fast every time we gathered. Our culture was built on trust and having fun. Picture yourself around a group of people that have only seen you when you are in a vulnerable state. These people only knew the version of you that was wild. The person that drank until they blacked out, or smoked until they fell asleep. Whoever you were in the middle of your days of addiction, is the only person they see when they run into you now. I want you to want better for yourself. This is not about impressing others or gaining the respect of an unsupportive family member. I want you to stay strong and know that this process is not easy. After years of doing the same thing, and thinking the same way, it can be tough to restart. But you are learning simultaneously. You know what it is like to hit rock bottom. Everyone operates differently. Every step you take, even if they are small, will eventually get you to your desired destination. Take note of this and remember, your addiction does not define you. Society might label you as an addict that will never succeed, but you can. Like I said before, it will take more than willpower and belief. Find at least one activity to reduce the anxiety that you have been feeling. The way you think is directly correlated to the way you act. See yourself from a different perspective. Instead of seeing the damage, you have done visible and invisible, see the growth. See yourself on the other side. Think about how you would feel if you got over the challenges. A recovered version of you is not that far away. Seek out the resources you need externally. Build relationships with those that can support you during the good, bad, and ugly stages. Addiction is not a life sentence. You have the choice every day to either stay in one position or challenge yourself to overcome. This could be a turning point in your life. What if you did what you said you wanted to do? How many opportunities can come from this? The opportunities are endless. You will gain experience from the highs and lows. Your character will be tested and you might want to quit. The part that people forget is the future benefits. Since we are so used to instant results, we quit at the first sign of adversity. Overcoming addiction does not come with next-day delivery. Save yourself some stress and know that there is not a button you can press. Instead of tracking the number of days, you have gone without 'fill in the blank', make the days count. Use a few hours a day to plan. Then execute that plan. See what works, discard what does not. Feed yourself with positive thoughts. Think about how far you have come, even if it is one day. Take it slow and speed up if you need to. Remind yourself, that your addiction does not define you. You got this. This is the road you are taking, do not stop.

CHAPTER 8

EGO

How do you feel when you walk into a room? Do you have good posture? Walking with your head high and shoulders back can make you appear more confident. Everyone stares at you because they are wondering why you look happy. They might think you are a cocky person. How could you possibly walk that tall with everything going on in the world? On the flip side, walking around with your back hunched over and your eyes down makes you appear less confident. You do not look sure of yourself. When people first meet you, they assume you are shy and passive. Why do you look so weak? Where is the strong sense of self? In this world, if you show too much confidence, then you are viewed as entitled and arrogant. If you are not carrying yourself with determination and poise, then people look at you with uncertainty. Ego is your sense of self-importance. This makes up your identity. In your mind, your ego determines what is real and not real. The word ego brings negativity to most people because they assume it is a horrible thing. Having a big ego has its pros and cons. On the positive side, you have high self-esteem. When you walk into a room, no matter where you are, you make your presence known. The dominance that you carry yourself with is established early. You have a strong sense of self that many people lack. A big ego drives you to be the best at everything you do. With that being said, you can learn to tone it down. In some situations that require you to learn more and retain information, you will need to get rid of the idea that you need no help. You have been convinced that it is every man for himself when the true power is found in a solid team. Now when a crisis hits and you have no one to turn to, then it would be alright to rely on yourself. This is less about denying the shark inside you and joining a school of fish. The focus is on being in tune with the inner shark that cannot stop moving forward. So how does this work? Where does having a big ego benefit you? Business. It is no secret that people in sales or leaders of a top-tier organization have bigger egos than most. When you are being sold a product or service, you want the seller to be confident. If they do not believe in themselves, then you do not feel the pressure to buy. The lack of clarity and direction makes you think you are donating and not a commitment. It is as if the seller is begging for your money in an unsure way. You would not give your money to a stranger. If that stranger is selling you something they do not believe in, then there is no way that you will take the bait. I will say that selling does not take energy from the ego. It does not take your whole ego to get the point across. From freshman year to senior year, my football team sold coupon cards. This was required in the summer. Each player took home twenty cards. The cards were given within the first week of summer workouts. So every player had a month to sell all the cards. Selling ten cards was mandatory. Every card was priced at twenty dollars. There were incentives for the number of cards sold. If you sold fifteen, you would get a shirt. Twenty cards would get the player a custom hoodie with their last name and number on it. Thirty or more cards would be gifts of an equal or greater value. This included earbuds, speakers, and other team gear. All four years, I sold over twenty cards. With the help of my parents, their colleagues, my neighbors, and friends. At the end of July, we would have a card blitz. This was the last day that all the cards we had were sold. Every position group had two leaders and they would pick underclassmen to join their team. When the groups were formed, the leaders got to pick a square on the grid. The grid was a map of Wichita. Going too far would mean we used more time driving than selling. Being close enough to reach the people that supported our team was the easy part. Even if they did not support our team we accepted donations. During my freshman and sophomore years, the group I was in both years did not sell much. Guys wanted to do their own thing. It was the end of the summer so why not take a break? If they already sold ten cards themselves, then why do they need to sell more? Every man was out to get theirs. Getting a hoodie was more important than helping the team. Now, I enjoyed getting hoodies and team gear. This is a slight exaggeration. But I say this to show you that our teams in 2017 and 2018 had too many guys with big egos. There is strength in numbers, yes, but if everyone is focused on "I" and not "we" then the team does not succeed. The card sales in the summer are not a direct correlation to the seasons that ended early. Nevertheless, it showed where their minds were at. This brings me to the cons of having a big ego. The major one is manipulation. Sometimes a big ego can make individuals play the victim card. Everything that goes wrong is not their fault. This person makes excuses as to why they cannot finish a task. They might try to make you feel bad for them. Another effect is judging. Instead of trying to learn more about a person, they assume. They judge everybody based on their looks alone. At the same time, they put their looks and abilities above everyone else. If you have ever been around someone judgmental, they are critical. It is to the point where it is excessive. Sometimes you have to use an objective view. But people who always have something negative to say are not the best to hang around. They drain the energy of the group. With these qualities, people will avoid you. When it comes to making plans or planning for a project, you will be one of the last people they contact. As a result, you stunt your growth. I am not talking about height or weight. It is the intangibles. These are your assets. In a business, intangible assets include brands, goodwill, trademarks, patents, and knowledge. You should start treating yourself like a business. What do you want your brand to look like? When people see you, what do you want them to notice? If you refuse to check your ego, then you are not learning. You are not in an uncomfortable position to grow. No knowledge of something brings assumptions and that is ignorance. When you have opportunities to soak in information from others and you ignore it, there is no excuse for future failure. You might end up wondering why you are spinning in circles instead of taking big leaps. Knowledge is power, that is not some overdone statement. Understanding that knowing without applying it is simply disrespecting your future self. Even if it is bad advice, you know what not to do. When you receive good advice, use it to keep moving. When I began taking lifting seriously, I would go to the gym with a couple of friends. We would look around and see bigger guys lifting heavier weights. So we decided to see if we could match them as far as intensity goes. Our pride took over. We did not want to look weak so we ego-lifted. Ego lifting is when someone lifts more weight than they should. The goal is to not look inferior and to impress others in the gym. The truth is, when everyone is focused on their workout, they do not care how much you lift. This can cause injury and limit your strength. Limited strength will bring gains to a halt. The pulled muscles and back pain are not worth it. Believe me. I have been through it. Thankfully, your body will tell you signs early that you are pushing too hard. Yes, it is possible. There is a difference between training smart while keeping the intensity and throwing all techniques out the window. I learned the hard way after loading too much weight on the bar for squat after a poor warmup. I was able to do five reps of the weight, but as soon as I reracked it, my back started hurting. The muscle stiffness makes it hard to walk. When you suffer from a back injury it forces you to use your hamstrings and hip flexors more. Other muscles are having to compensate for the lack of stability. What I learned from people with more experience was this. When working out, you can still see some gains when you lift lighter weights with more reps. This is called hypertrophy. It is when you increase the number of sets and reps to increase the size of the muscle. Maybe it feels good to try to go for a max every time you lift, but from my experience, that has only made me feel weaker. Like any workout, the results vary. Many factors go into building the right gym routine. Having a big ego in the gym will rob you of your strength gains. No matter what, you should not look to impress others; impress yourself. Exceed your expectations. Failing to control your ego will make you more impulsive. This is your id. The id is the part of your mind that is responsible for instincts and impulses. It focuses on your instincts. Your personality is made up and your beliefs are developed. The id controls your behavior and it starts at birth. It is the first part of you that is established. Through influences, your ego and super-ego are developed. Individuals with a closer connection to their identity are more likely to work on themselves with a positive attitude. When they face a problem with their behavior, they adapt quicker than those who are less connected. Therefore, those who are impulsive and cannot control their behavior tend to be more destructive. This is the difference between a child knocking down cereal boxes in an aisle versus grabbing the one they want and holding it up to their parent. Some common impulsive behaviors are binge drinking, gambling, and drugs. Being active in these three areas will cause you to become more violent. Your aggression will be used to satisfy what you want now instead of building your future. When you are out of your element, you will feel different. I am pushing you to leave your comfort zone. However, you must have some discernment when it comes to the places you go and the people you spend time with. This is where you should judge. The ego whispers in your ear, "you can hang with these people", "take another drink, you can handle it", and "it is just one bet, what do you have to lose?." Your ability to judge well will be put to the test if it has not already. If you have ever been somewhere you were not supposed to be, it probably felt good at the moment, but then the gut feeling comes in. You start to feel like something is off. Depending on the transportation you took and the people you are around, you might have to ride it out. You might have to stay in that spot for a little while longer. The only hope is not making a decision that changes your life for the worse. When you are surrounded by people who binge drink, you are more likely to binge drink too. We do not like to be the odd man out or be picked last for teams. Our ego steers us in the wrong direction. It might feel like you have no control over this but you do. Mentally, you need to be the driver, not the passenger. Critical thinking is vital to your growth in this world. Where does this ability come from? It comes from your super-ego. The super-ego is your conscience. It is the part in your mind that highlights critical thinking. As a child, controlled or not, you based the moves you made on influencers. With every year, you gained new values. People older than you like teachers, coaches, and parents are responsible for this. If you are older, maybe you have placed the blame on them for the way you are today. If you were only taught a certain way from one lens, then it is hard to see life from a different perspective. I want you to know that this is not easy for anyone. We like to receive answers that only line up with our beliefs. When we are challenged, we sometimes feel less than. The younger you are, the smoother the process is when it comes to solidifying morals. Including influencers who are useful to the raunchy and dreadful ones. You are born into a "monkey see, monkey do" situation. You will learn if you have not already, that you do not always have to "do." This takes discipline, just like anything you want to accomplish. Think about how you felt when you reached a goal that was on your mind for a long time. This is pride; the satisfaction you get from achieving something. You can also feel pride when someone else reaches a goal or when your favorite team wins a championship. Pride can help you motivate others to be their best. Due to the amount of confidence you have in yourself, you can give that same confidence to others. You feel a sense of responsibility, and that drives you. When you are working on your passion simultaneously, you can practice gratitude. The joy is spread, you walk a little taller, and you are committed to yourself. All this is honorable, but too much pride can make you self-centered. Everything you do is only done to benefit you. Instead of serving others, you always look at what you could get out of it. When you are truly, actively helping you do not look for anything in return. Therefore, those who are extremely prideful tend to believe everything they say or do is right. They refuse to be corrected. Forming relationships with them is an uphill battle. But there is a chance to get rid of this. At the least, the pride will still be there but not at a higher level. The opposite of pride is humility. Humility is viewing yourself with modesty; being humble. Being humble allows you to acknowledge your strengths without being full of yourself. It keeps the ego balanced. As a result of humility, your patience grows. Once you have reached a healthy level of humility, you can teach others how to be humble. Every team I played for has been humbled at least once. Sometimes it would be losing a game to a team you know deep down you should have beat. Other times it was the loss of chemistry on the field and court. In tournaments, after winning two or three games, we would make the semifinals. From a basketball perspective, it was clear that opponents were tougher the further we moved. The last game before the championship is usually the hardest. After blowing out teams we faced before, we have a sense of entitlement. Because we won game two versus team X, there is no way we could lose the semifinal to team Y. It is one thing to lose early in the playoffs, but it is another thing to lose in the championship game. The emotions hit harder because you traveled all that distance, practiced for hours, to fall short. Part of the reason this happens is pride. We spread the mentality that the game is already won and all we have to do is play. This usually ends in a loss that could have been avoided. On the contrary, being too humble has its consequences. Low self-esteem can lead you to feel undeserving of success. Similar to the ego, you might come off as a spineless, nervous person or team. With too much humidity, it can be harder to get what you want. You do not have to be a doormat. Too much pride can block you from giving value to others. Receiving is pleasant while giving is not always an attractive move. The fulfillment you get from being on your purpose is unmatched. In your humility, you believe you can accomplish anything you put your mind to without degrading others. In competition, you respect your opponents because they could beat you at any time. Keep your pride and humility balanced. It is like a non-alcoholic Arnold Palmer. The lemonade represents pride and the tea is humility. When the lemonade overpowers the drink, you can tell right away. When tea is the dominant component, there is no tang. Having said that, you need to know how to check your ego and practice humility. If you want to deal with your ego, you must look introspectively. Look inside yourself. Get rid of the need to be in control all the time. Trying to control everything will drive you crazy. Admit when you are wrong. Then take ownership when you are wrong. This takes the weight off and more people will respect you for being honest. At the same time, this allows you to forgive others that have similar qualities. Wherever you are, the doors you walk through, the rooms you meet in, it is important to check your ego. When you are on a team and you lose a game, it is easy to play the blame game. Everyone is pointing fingers. There is usually the one player that gets defensive when he or she is called out. This can harm an athlete more if they compete in an individual sport. Your ego can be crushed when you play golf or tennis because you are on an island. There is no one to blame but you. You are more likely to make a change when you admit your faults. When people take the time to hold you accountable, it motivates you to fix it. For humility, you need to know your strengths and weaknesses. Know that you are stronger in some areas and need coaching in other areas. When you are driven by your pride, you start boasting about all you can do. But what about the things you cannot do? A quick solution would be not to brag at all. Think about who you are trying to reach. Why try to win the hearts of people you do not care about? This is a waste of time. You might think they will feel inadequate, but most of them do not care. Nobody likes to work on their weaknesses because they make mistakes. People fail to realize that mistakes are a part of the process. If it was a clear road with flowers and sunshine, then no one would be seeking help. Due to your beliefs and values growing more rooted as you get older, you need to be open to new ideas. The prejudice you carry can steal the potential experience you accumulate over time. Think of prejudice as pre-judging. Being judgmental will not allow you to be fully present. The doubts start to set in, and you will not grow as fast as you want. Connectivity with social media and news is in our faces each day. It seems like the more you seek attention, the more successful you get. This is not true. People will do anything for a quick period of fame. If you are actively working on yourself, you will not need to seek attention. The results will speak for you. Last but not least, gratitude. It is easy to tell people what you are grateful for around a dinner table on Thanksgiving, but what about the rest of the year? You certainly do not wait a whole year to show your gratitude. There are times in your years that you practiced gratitude without knowing it. If you want to make a conscious effort in this practice, then you can journal. Now I know what you are thinking. You live a busy life, you have kids to care for and obligations to tend to. Excuses are not your friends, so stop relying on them. Grab a journal, or a piece of paper and write down five to ten things you are grateful for. You can do this once and put it on the refrigerator to remind you. Another way is to do this once a month. By the end of every month, you can look back at the different things you listed. If you are involved in new activities and building new relationships, then every list will be distinctive. In July of 2021, I bought a journal. I found the time to write weekly. Five minutes before bed, or during your lunch break at work, you can make time too. It is okay to have pride while being humble. Have some pride in the work you have done so far. Consider the future growth. Use your ego as energy to propel you forward. You connect with your identity more by identifying your values. Making choices will not take as long because you are drawn to what lines up with the values. Take some time to write or meditate. When you receive praise, keep improving. Do not walk around boasting about your achievements. Although, there is nothing wrong with showing your progress. Your ego never leaves you. An individual might be on the extreme side of humility, not recognizing their success. One can also be egotistical to the point of toxicity. While your life will be far from balanced, it will help you later on when you can channel both sides. Give yourself some credit. Do not dismiss your efforts. The passions you go after will reassure your authenticity. You are no longer faking it to make it. Pretending to be successful can only get you so far. People like stories about those that kept going, the ones that did the dirty work. What you do in the dark will come to light. The choices might not be exposed right now, but the results will show. Whether you put in the work or not, people will notice. In addition to the inner voice that tells you that you are not good enough, there is a voice that believes in you. This is a part of your id. The voice should push you. You move according to your sense of self. Through experience, you gain confidence. After completing one step, your motivation grows. You want to do more and cross every finish line you set before yourself. Driven people seem to be more attractive. They have structure and direction. This type of person has the potential to be an efficient leader. Teammates and coworkers like this are fun to be around. More often than not, the energy is positive. They check their egos at the door and focus on the job that needs to be done. As far as identity goes, they are not all over the place. Through dark times, this person appears to have it all together. A tight connection with this person will make room for improvements in your life. You might start to mimic them when it comes to challenges. At the end of the day, I want you to be able to say that you stayed honest with yourself. This might not happen consistently, but if you are making the effort, then it will eventually compound. Your ego, super-ego, and id make up your personality. Take time to work on your identity. If you feel like you do not need to work on it, great. But do not complain when you face resistance. Take ownership and take control of your life.

CHAPTER 9

DIET

You need to go on a diet. Before you jump to conclusions, we need to break it down. What we eat and drink habitually is our diet. This can also be interpreted as the act of avoiding certain foods and drinks. In fitness, there are many different types of diets. The well-known methods are intermittent fasting, keto, paleo, veganism, and carnivore. I have never tried any of these diets. But I have heard the pros and cons of each. When I got into lifting weights consistently, I found that the diet affects the gains. It might not be as direct, but it is a strong factor. Three basic strategies are bulking, maintaining, and cutting. Bulking is essentially eating a calorie surplus. The number of calories per day has to exceed your average amount consumed regularly. What worked for me was structure. The primary meals; breakfast, lunch, and dinner must have the most calories. If you want to put on weight without dropping off, four to six meals are preferable. I am not a professional. This is what worked for me. One high-protein snack in between each of these meals will help you. To grow even bigger on the scale, you can eat a snack before bed to go into the next day with more energy. In a season of bulking, you should look to add more carbs, red meats, and poultry to your plate. This is not a cookbook but meals that included eggs, oatmeal, chicken breast, rice, and steak were my favorites. Two years ago, I found an app that helped me track my weight and daily caloric intake. When I was bulking, I was consuming around 4,200 calories daily. By the end of the day, my goal was to eat 50% carbs, 30% fats, and 20% protein. Now for those that are new to fitness, that might sound extreme. At first, it took some adjusting because I was considering everything I ate. I had to enter every item. This was not as hard as I thought. I weighed in every Monday. At one point I was gaining around half a pound to one pound weekly. There is the dirty bulk where you eat everything in sight, including fast food and desserts. I went on a clean bulk. The nutrient-dense foods gave me enough energy for my workouts. My body responded in a great way. I adjusted to the new weight that I put on. The second strategy is maintaining. Even though you put on weight, you need to learn how to keep that weight and the gains you made in the process. When I was maintaining, I ate fewer calories than before. I was consuming around 4000 calories daily. The intensity was the same when lifting. Putting on weight was and still is exciting to me. Being able to lift more and hit personal records is stimulating. This drove me to try heavier weights that I did not imagine lifting before. My hydration was also a priority. Without it, the movements would be poor. The struggles I faced were keeping up with the calories and doing cardio without losing weight. After changing some of the foods I ate, I was able to find something that worked for me. Cutting was never hard for me. When you are younger, your metabolism is faster. The only change I made to my routine was more cardio and more hydration. I ate more protein bars for snacks. From freshman year to senior year of high school, I gained forty pounds. Two years later I put on twenty pounds. I will say that in the cutting phase, you will be more vascular and leaner. Losing weight was what I disliked the most. It felt like I was getting weaker. But this was a result called body recomposition when the fat percentage goes down while building muscle. I am sharing this because fitness has been important to me for years. Being physically fit is great. Eating the right foods to stay healthy takes discipline. But eating and drinking are not the only parts that make up your diet. There is a mental side. Take the content you watch for example. Streaming platforms are bringing in hundreds of millions in profit from people across the world. You can become an individual of high value based on the content you watch. YouTube has content that can help you be a better cook, musician, and photographer, the possibilities are endless. Websites that specialize in learning new skills are also available. When used correctly, in six months to a year you could change your life. After learning a new skill, or mastering the one you currently have, you can increase your income and meet new people on the way up. Everyone wants change, but no one wants to change. Learning a new skill, creating something valuable, or adding value to your work is not a popular task. People complain about their lives but do nothing about it. The resources are out there, you have to put in the work. No one is going to do it for you. A negative side to content is the kind that brings you down. Content that takes away your time and energy. The type that causes anxiety. News channels that do not line up with your political beliefs, adult sites, unorthodox tv shows; and everything similar. On social media, you are marketing yourself, a business, or both. What are you liking and reposting? Who do you follow? Be honest with yourself. Keeping up with celebrities does not make your dreams come true. Are you spreading positivity and lifting others? Or are you getting into arguments in the comment section? Are you degrading others, making them feel worse? We are all guilty. Realistically, we rarely consider this. Especially if you were born after these apps were created. In nutrition, there are different types of cleanses you can go on. There is the juice cleanse, avoiding certain foods, colon cleanse, and liver detox. When it comes to social media, I like to do a follower cleanse. Across all platforms, I take the time to look at everyone I follow. If you follow over one thousand people, this can be tedious. I weed out people that do not add value or new information to my life. For accounts that only spread negativity, I unfollow immediately. I have done this at least three times a year. This does not have to be a monthly activity, but if that works for you, then go for it. Furthermore, who and what you listen to are equally important. Who are you listening to? Do you only value the voices that reinforce your opinions? The music that gets you ready to the podcasts that inspire you. Content creators that you are loyal to; it matters. From birth, you cannot speak. Instead, you listened, and watched. Who you are today is an accumulation of the people who taught you and the actions you took in response. The voices surround you daily. What are you letting in? What are you letting out? What does the pressure feel like? Maybe you grew up with parents that had high expectations. So the love you received was contingent upon your achievements. On the flip side, maybe you did not receive any support. So you worked to win people over by reaching your goals. There are many voices in your life that you should listen to and ones you should completely ignore. Coaches tell you what you are doing wrong and what you can do to fix those issues. Doctors give you medicine recommendations to heal what is bothering you. Religious leaders share their testimonies. Therapists allow you to speak so they can listen and search through solutions. Financial advisors let you know if you are under budget or spending excessively. Mentors give you the blueprint, but it is up to you to make it fit your goals. The elderly give you advice and recall unforgettable events in their lives. People ahead of you might flaunt their items. At the same time, people doing worse than you are showing gratitude for what they have. They could be inspired by you. A stranger might support you more than a family member. Someone is watching you, listening to you too. Children repeat some of the words and phrases their parents use. Sometimes curse words come out. But it is not their fault. They are living in an environment where people have bad language. This can cause the child to keep using those words throughout years of schooling. While cursing in the house is not the worst thing a parent can do, it has its effects. Around the age of ten, children start to develop their values. One decade later, those values are usually solidified. Most people are familiar with the crucial years and the changes that take place. We have all gone through it. If you are younger and have not yet, then the time is coming. Technology has bombarded us with sounds and voices from every angle of every situation. Platforms make it easy to voice your opinion no matter who it offends. Our attention is being demanded every day. The noise can get so loud that we forget about the work that needs to be done. Watch what you listen to. Moreover, what you read is a part of your diet as well. What are you reading? What are you reading into? Maybe the news articles from biased websites are not the most reliable. But they seem interesting because of their radical ideas. The comment section underneath a political post is not the best standard you should base your opinions on. Millions of people like to get a word in about every issue that crosses their timeline. What does your feed look like? It is easy to get caught up in reading what only supports your beliefs. Opposing views must be recognized. You might find that looking at something from a different perspective can open up your mind. Reading allows you to step into the mind of the author; you might learn something life-changing. One of the overlooked parts of your daily consumption is your circle. You are who you hang around. For some that might be a tough pill to swallow, but it is the truth. A group should not be wishy-washy. If you want to reach a certain level of success, you must be around positive influences. This might sound familiar if a parent or teacher ever told you to hang around these types of people. As you get older, you will understand. You need people to hold you accountable. At some point, you should get tired of the lies you tell yourself. A functional group is full of individuals that add value to each other. This is your unstoppable team. The people on your team remind you to stay humble when you are at the top of the mountain. They recognize your achievements and want you to keep going. Wins and losses are shared. Everyone goes through struggles in this process, so having people to talk to is critical. When you meet, you make smart decisions. No one is left behind, arrested, or seriously injured. Now, these situations might sound silly, but they can happen. These people celebrate when you reach a goal. You do the same. Whenever you decide to try a new business venture, they are rooting for you. As a member, you have the choice to share your goals, though I do not recommend telling multiple people. What you can do is put in the work, then show off your results. But if you are a tight-knit group, then this will drive the levels of accountability upward. Now that they know what you want to accomplish, they will be waiting to see if you can do it. This is not saying they do not believe in you, but once it is out there, you are doing a disservice not to execute. Unlike most people, everyone in this group should have a growth mindset. A fixed mindset is an anchor; a crutch. What happens in dysfunctional groups is envy. One person veers and chases their dream. They come back to the group and everyone is jealous of what they worked for. Instead of congratulating them, they are disgusted. They feel left out. Individuals who are living their purpose and coming together are a beacon of inspiration. No jealousy exists because every time you win, they feel like they won too. Every time you lose, they do their best to pick you up. This is a continuous process. Authenticity and trust should be the main pillars of your circle. The process of chasing what you want can be taxing on the mind which affects the body. If your life was a movie, who would your supporting cast be? Every award-winning film had a strong main character and a powerful supporting cast. Emphasis on the supporting. It is not called a degenerate cast or a failing cast. With an above-average supporting cast, you can do incredible things. Additionally, you return the favor. In the beginning, you might experience some pain because people are holding you to your word, but the gains are unrivaled. This can take you far in life. Still, people do not take this seriously, and they end up on the other side. A dysfunctional group contains people that live for the weekend. The jobs they are working have nothing to do with their dreams. A dead-end job is not allowing them to be on their purpose. On a side tangent, they could be the ones that are temporarily working so they can get to that next level. But those people are actively taking steps. When you only look forward to the weekend, you are in a constant loop of instant gratification and sadness. From Monday to Thursday, you are counting down the days. For starters, members make poor decisions. Every waking hour they chase the next high. Alcohol, drugs, sex, and more. They rely on these activities. As if it could not get worse, they eat fast food all the time and have poor hygiene. Fitness is avoided, and they are not productive outside the house. They carry a negative attitude that is contagious in the workplace. Any slight change in their life sets them off. Being around them is a chore. When you try to correct them they get defensive. Since they never checked their ego, they do not see what they can control. From what I have seen, this group always has one person that does not belong there. This is a good thing. The one person is talented but they run with the wrong crowd. They go down a comfortable path and only gain new addictions. If they had a reason why they were after greatness, then they lose it. The envy grows if this person deviates from the false values of the group. They have been lied to. Unfortunately, the only way they learn is by hitting rock bottom. From an optimistic lens, the only way they can go is up. But the process is ugly. Letting go of destructive habits that have been ingrained for years is tough. I applaud anyone who has come out of this dark place. You are stronger than you think. The question you are probably asking yourself is this.What can I do today? What is something that I can apply right now? Take inventory of your circle. There are five questions that I ask myself. What value do they bring? How do I feel around these people? If they are making me worse, what do I need to do? If they are making me better, how do I keep this going? Then add or subtract based on the answers you get. You need to know whether the foundation is purpose or pleasure. Look at every person objectively. This is the one time you can. Avoid sugar-coating because you will deceive yourself. If you are wondering how often you should do this, there is no right answer. The answer is found when you feel like you are going down the wrong path. On the other hand, you could be blessed with ambitious friends. Life moves fast. Evaluating as often as possible can be stressful. The burned bridges and new connections will be worth your time. Professionally, you can sit down as a group and ask uncomfortable questions. For instance, a question like "What are we doing with our lives?" This will stir the pot and allow each person to look inward. This is not putting yourself above them as you adopted their behaviors too. Do not be afraid to step on toes. When they see how much you care, it might drive them to be better. If they do not support it, then they are satisfied where they are. Every lazy habit will soon catch up to them if it has not already. The right people will come into your life when you stay focused. Why wait? If you hang around people who are not ambitious, do not expect a high return on your investment. Be aware. When you are younger, it is easier to leave them because you go your separate ways. As an older individual, you will find it hard to go down the path of discomfort. Leaving behind everyone you know might be terrifying. Eventually, you will have to. Going back to technology, there were a few challenges that harmed my growth. I was addicted to social media. Every time I went on, I would scroll for hours. My sleep schedule was off because of this. The dopamine rush had to be stronger each time. I set time limits on the apps that I used the most. These apps were not serving me. At the least, my consumption was mindless; there was no benefit. The main app that I was using constantly was Instagram. So I deleted it for thirty days. When the month passed without using Instagram, it took me a few more days to redownload it. During this time between the end and the reinstallation, I only logged on through my computer. Surprisingly, I did not feel the need to check the other apps as much. My feelings were not based on what I was on my feed. What I learned was this; I was more present in the virtual world than in the real world. The longer I stayed off social media, the more focused I was. A fire was lit inside me to push harder and dig deeper. I saw people living the life that I dreamed of. Instead of acting as I did before with envy, I looked at it as, "I could be there someday." This caused me to stop scrolling and start planning. When I got done planning, I started doing. Thinking you are going to be successful is great, but the doers are the ones that get there. This is what I wanted. Success can be faked on these apps, making the average person feel worthless. The world separates the winners and losers. Losers have the time to put in the work but do nothing. Every setback paralyzes them into a state of complacency. No determination and no fight in them. Then there are winners. Winners take their losses as lessons. They do not let themselves stay on the ground, even if they fell thousands of times. With every closed door, they look for another door with opportunities ready to be taken. What I learned from the thirty-day hiatus was I was stronger than I thought. Too often we try something new and immediately think we will fail at it. Good. Failing teaches you. Accept the fact that you have to learn. I believed that I needed these connections to let people know I was still alive. How foolish of me. Right? Nobody noticed I took a break. This is the beauty of it, nobody has to notice. You do not have to tell anybody, but you can let them see how you have changed since then. Honestly, the important people in your life should have your phone number or email. Anyone else will be temporarily disconnected. This is okay. Sometimes you need to unplug yourself. If you feel alone, there is always a way to reconnect. You do not have to be chained to your distractions. There is one common theme with every successful person I have met. This is something that you will see when you meet these people too. It is their morning routine. Win the day by starting in the morning. Win in the morning by preparing the night before. If it sounds simple to you, then it is. A routine does not have to be complicated by any means. What time do you go to bed? What time do you fall asleep? Using screens within an hour before bed can make you lose track of time. One more video, one more episode, one more post. The time adds up quickly. Do you feel exhausted in the middle of the day? Do you find it hard to go to sleep? Great. I did too. If you are an adult you should find the amount of sleep you get between seven to nine hours. What worked for me was seven to seven and a half hours. Sometimes if I got too much sleep, I would feel fatigued. Once you have your sleep mastered, move on to your first actions. Make your bed. As a kid, my bed was always checked to see if it was made. I did not realize the importance of this until later, which is normal for kids that ignore their parents. When you make your bed, there is potential to be more productive throughout the day. There is a domino effect. Think about the following statement. If you can make your bed, you can conquer anything thrown at you every day. I use my phone as an alarm. As soon as I hear the sound, I get up and turn it off. Hitting snooze can ruin your mentality. It makes you want to avoid responsibilities. You cannot hit the snooze button on life. What do you do after you wake up? Checking messages and social media can make you more anxious before your day starts. The amount of instant information entering your brain early can keep you dragging along. What you do when you wake up is important. One trick that I tried was counting down from five and jumping out of bed as if I was late to an event. My feet hit the ground at zero. My alarms are turned off, I take a sip of water, and start getting dressed. Counting down from five works for me. For you, it might be ten. Some days I say it out loud, other days I say it in my head. It works. Try it for one week, and see how much you get done. Similar to the breaks you take from various forms of media, you will not feel inclined to check the apps on your phone. The night before, you will turn the tv off earlier and set your clothes out for the next day. You can track your sleep too. For a month you can track your sleep, then compare it to your productivity. On days with less productivity, you might be getting too little or too much sleep. It is up to you to find that medium. Stay consistent with it, if it gives you the desired level of productivity. I am not telling you to be perfect. Nobody is. Life happens and sometimes we get sleep deprived. It might not be sleep. Perhaps, there is something else holding you back. The beliefs, your attitude, and your thoughts are controllable. The thoughts turn into actions. Who is around you when you are taking action? Spend time with people that actively bring positivity into your life. Refrain from associating with those who repeatedly participate in degenerate activities. You have compassion. Do not waste your energy on those who do not want to change. Chances are if you run around with snakes, you will get bit sooner or later. Adopt the habits that fit your future. Acknowledge the mistakes you have made so far, then forgive yourself. Among others who fail to take control, you are different. Take the lead. This is your life. On this path, this is your chance to put yourself first in a healthy way. It does not mean you lack compassion for others. To reach a greater level of service to others, you need to be familiar with what you put in your mind, body, and spirit.

Make sure the voices you listen to are reliable. Judge your circle. This is okay to do. Unfollow accounts that bring your spirit down. Throw away the foods that are not helping you reach your fitness goals. No one is above this. I am not above this. The value you provide to others is bigger than you. Of course, you will get something out of the work you put in. At the same time, you must have the right mentality. If you believe you can do anything you put your mind to, then it will not be a problem. Stop telling yourself lies. Do not forge success, it will come back to humble you. Be the supporting cast member for those in your group, as they are supporting you. Thus, everyone should go on a diet. Take into account everything you consume. Build a healthy morning routine. Be an active member in your circle, family, and community who is changing for the better. Know your diet. Know yourself.

CHAPTER 10

WAR ON LUST

W hat is the war on lust? It looks like a play on words from the War on Drugs. Although that campaign has been going on for decades, this chapter is not about that. From an early age, we all experience a desire for something. A five-year-old may be asking for a new bike or stuffed animal, while a fifteen-year-old wants a new car. But what is lust? What does this have to do with you and me? Lust in its simplest definition is an intense sexual desire or appetite. What you need to know is that lust is not just sexual. But that is the main interpretation when brought up. One can participate in the over-indulgence of food and drinks, also known as gluttony. In the sexual sense, lust can cause people to search for partners that fit their fantasies and not their desired future. It whispers in the ears of its victim and convinces them to go forward. The situations that come from this are far from positive. Unhealthy habits can be born and debilitate a person for years. There are lighter forms of lust, but the ones that will be covered are sex, money, and power. All three terms seem to be ordinary, which is not a problem. Living in abundance is great, it is peaceful, but it becomes a problem when overused. People become ill, face chronic problems, and fail in their relationships. If you are familiar with Shakespeare, all that glitters is not gold. Just because it looks and feels good, does not mean it is your best option. A piece of chocolate cake every once in a while is not harmful. Combing this with an inactive lifestyle and overeating and you might be looking at a future with diabetes. If you want to maintain the physique you worked so hard for in the gym, then a twelve-pack of beer should not be in your refrigerator. Opening the door each day, and seeing the beer, will soon make you want to drink. Say you finished a great workout, it is nighttime. One beer does not kill you. Right? Who says no to one beer? Well, do it long enough and it turns into a habit. It turns into an instant reward for going hard in the gym. Now every time you workout, you feel the need to drink after. One beer might not be feeling as good, so you drink two, then four. Eventually, you are consuming so much that you need something with more potency. After quite some time, you hit an all-time low. This is not what you wanted from the beginning. All you wanted was a release, a reward for the hard work you have been putting in. You convinced yourself that you deserve it. When it comes to lust, the first part of the definition is an intense sexual desire. So where does the desire come from? What is something in this world that is free from the cost of mental health? The answer is pornography. Sexually explicit photos, videos, and other content are used to arouse the viewer. If it was not already made clear, this is a highly addictive form of instant gratification. Before the internet, you had to go to a store to purchase content. Or you had to search for magazines around the house. Now, it is accessible through an internet connection. Similar to nicotine and alcohol, not everyone is an addict. But the earlier you start, the harder it is to leave that lifestyle. When viewing porn, people masturbate. If you are engaging in a pleasurable activity, the reward system in our brains releases an insane amount of dopamine. Each time we do it, we remember how great the said activity makes us feel. The brain writes the script of our past emotions and patterns that turn into behaviors. According to society, porn is not a bad thing, and masturbation is normal. Some call it healthy because it reduces stress. In my humblest opinion, that could not be further from the truth. Just as it was described in the beer example, overstimulation causes us to seek more porn that is violent. Unfortunately, your brain cannot tell the difference between sex with a real person and the release from porn. When you start to increase your tolerance, you are also increasing the amount of dosage. Regrettably, we tell ourselves lies when we watch porn. In your mind, it might sound like, "It is only one picture", "Just one photo", "I have been doing good so I'll just masturbate", "Nobody will know", and "I'll quit after this time." The truth is not always pleasant. It does not have to be. Sometimes the truth knocks you down, other times it wakes you up. The lies are comfortable. Is porn getting you closer to your dreams? Is it strengthening your relationships? Could you quit right now if you tried? How many days would you last? Here is a reality check; if porn was helping you, then you would not be seeking help! The shame would not be present if it served you. You would have stronger relationships if there were benefits. In 2000, Ron DeHaas founded Covenant Eyes. This is a software company that provides people with protection and community while resisting the temptation of porn. On their website, they have alarming statistics about this issue. These stats should wake you up if you are addicted, or near addiction. In their studies, they found that 28,258 users are watching pornography every second. Around $3,075.64 is spent on porn every second. As far as the scenes go, 88% of them show physical aggression, and 49% show verbal aggression. The vast majority, 90% of teens and 96% of young adults are neutral and accepting of it when they talk to their friends. So this does not discriminate when it comes to age. From a wide range, you are subject to people who believe this is not a problem. Therefore, it can be hard to find that support group when you are struggling. I advise you to check out their website as well as other resources. These are just a few statistics. The rest will shock you. Some of the studies are just a few years old. The numbers might be higher, which is not the direction we need to go in society. When you find the information that you are looking for, you might feel hopeless. Porn promotes human trafficking and child sexual abuse. People receive unnatural views of sex and how relationships work. If you feel like you are in too deep, you are not. In the last decade, there have been new organizations and apps that tackle this addiction. Do not believe you are alone. If you struggle with this, there is a community of people that will welcome you with open arms. The resources are there for you. In this world, sex is promoted everywhere. If you believe it is not, pay attention to the new shows and movies that have been released. Look at the commercials and even cartoons that are flooding the screen. Think about social media. No matter where you look, someone or something is being sexualized. It is right in your face and it could be hard to resist. Porn was made to be hard to resist and keep you chained. The mindset changes when you leave this so-called normal way of living. This is a part of our lives, but it does not have to be a part of yours. You can break free. The future relationships you get into do not have to be tainted by pornography or any other sexually immoral activity. It is not worth your mental health, energy, and time. Unrealistic standards are being set by the companies that benefit from the consumption. If you are wondering where else you can find a community that will assist you on your journey of recovery, try NoFap. Alexander Rhodes, the founder of NoFap, is a former addict. Fapping is another word for masturbation. This website was founded in 2011. It is a movement that is still fairly new and people discover it in times of need. Maybe it is out of desperation, but it is better than not seeking assistance. I bring attention to this topic because it is often swept under the rug. Luckily, more content creators inform the public holistically. If you are addicted, leaving pornography can and will change your life. The urges will always be there. Biologically, we are meant to have these feelings. This is why it is important to identify your triggers. When you are on social media and see provocative images, be careful. Your thoughts will change the way you see them. If you are out in public, it might make you look at people as objects and not human beings. In a similar way that your brain recorded patterns of destructive habits, you can rewire it in recovery. Do not expect to be fully recovered after one day. If you have been at it for years, then your healing process will not happen overnight. For some, they might have been introduced unwillingly, and that is unfortunate. You might not have gotten yourself in this situation from the beginning, but it is up to you to change. Nobody deserves to be trapped in the endless cycle of shame. My only hope is that this is talked about more. The awareness needs to be heightened. Our addiction has contributed to this billion-dollar industry built on exploitation. As technology evolves, virtual reality is already being used as a tool to keep us under the spell. No matter what your status is with pornography, you can contribute to the recovery process of the youth and adults who need it. So far, we have covered sexual attraction and how negative it has become in society. What else needs to be addressed? Money and power. Naturally, it is the default to say you want more money. We can agree that most people want to be financially free from debt. Nobody wants to live in poverty or go broke. The culture today is pushing the mindset of greed. Wanting to provide for your family in the future is great. The dream of raising your own family without having to worry about funds is tremendous. But if you are obsessed with getting more money, it becomes a problem. Like it or not, we all have dealt with this. I want to introduce you to this lifestyle called flex culture. Flex culture is the purchasing of goods or services to look the wealthiest out of your friends and family. The outlet for this is social media. Posts usually contain expensive products like shoes, clothes, and accessories. In addition to this, people flaunt their money by showing off foreign vehicles, watches, and jewelry. Contrary to what we see in music videos and movies, flexing does not make you friends. If it does, then they are your friends for the wrong reasons. Too many people fall into the trap of spending money they do not have to impress people they do not like. As soon as their income goes up by one thousand or ten thousand, they immediately start shopping for new items. Why? We feel the need to gratify ourselves. We have been tricked into putting ourselves on a pedestal so that others can be jealous. Nearly identical to lust, greed is an excessive desire for possession and wealth. Notice how it is not a regular desire or inspirational desire; it is an excessive desire. Flexing is not at all the worst you could do. When individuals have been working for years to reach their dreams, it is nice to see how far they have come. When flexing is done to belittle people that do not earn as much, then it becomes an issue. What does this do to the teen or young adult on social media? They continue to scroll through posts wondering if they are valued. We start to compare ourselves to people ahead of us. If we lack the possessions that they have, we start to envy them. We become discontent. Our gratitude drops and now we are in a race to look rich. We need to stop comparing ourselves to others. It ruins your self-esteem. Nothing good comes from this; it is like you are bringing your value down and invalidating your efforts. What is better than looking rich? Being rich of course. But that is not the same for everyone. We all have our definitions. Maybe the word rich to you means rich in spirit. Having the ability to raise a family with healthy children is a blessing. Owning a business that builds generational wealth is impressive. Having the means to donate to charities and organizations with causes that you believe in is great. Being financially literate no matter where the economy stands is an advantage. Obsessing what you do not have makes you forget what you do have. Growing up, I was told to count my blessings. Not all of my friends had both parents and a supportive family. Some people were bussed into school for four consecutive years. A few of my friends came from broken homes in rough areas. On the other hand, some always had new shoes, phones, and cars. I applaud anyone who is actively changing the narrative of their last name. Call it dysfunction, call it a generational curse; there is always one person that pulls their family out of the dark. We have the decision to use our time and money wisely. Money can always be earned while time is not guaranteed. So who am I to flex what is temporary? What do I look like when I degrade others for not 'being on my level'? Greed is powerful and it is running rampant in society. While many goods and services are in scarcity, we must stop believing there is not enough for everybody. When it comes to opportunities, it is clear that they are not for everyone. However, you can create a mindset of abundance. How do you accomplish this? Your thoughts. This might be a pointless exercise but think about your thoughts. Like I have said before, you are not your past. The bad memories do not need to be at the forefront of your life. Some of these thoughts are intrusive and unwanted at random times. But you can cultivate abundance through your mind. I will say this again because it has extraordinarily helped me. Practice gratitude. You do not have x,y, or z but you do have a,b, and c. Accept that it is okay to be hungry for more while still being grateful. The resentment and anger toward those who are successful are unhealthy. Hating on others does not serve you; people that hate on you do not serve you. When you look at what you want out of life and say to yourself, "I can work my way up to that point" it gives you a boost of confidence. Believe that there is no limit to your success. Just because you reach a higher level, does not mean you cannot continue to grow. At this time with new technology and resources, there is an abundance of opportunities in any field you explore. Instead of believing that only people born into wealthy families can be successful, start searching for opportunities. Sitting around all day liking posts is not taking action. Stop comparing, get up and do something about it. After sticking to this mindset, you will start to win. More money will be earned while more relationships form. If the people you are with care about what is in your bank account, then you should not associate with them. Especially if they are lacking in this area, it is best to avoid them. Envy is dangerous. When you have made it out of a terrible situation through hard work, and you start rising from the eighty percent to the twenty and ten; people start to feel entitled. They believe since they know you, they deserve a little money on the side. The only contribution they made to your success is their judgment. But there are two sides to this. Giving back to those that helped you get to a certain point is a feeling that everyone should experience. Although, there is joy in receiving; giving seems to be more fulfilling. Once you reach a level of financial security, you can bless people for no reason. Have you ever been in a drive-thru and the person in front of you pays for your meal? Even if the total cost was $1.28, that felt good, right? Maybe they drove off without needing a "thank you", they just did it. This brightens your day, especially when they are not doing it for attention. You do not need to help everybody. It is not your job to save the world. But you can start in your community. Money allows procedures in the hospital to be done and gives food to the hungry, and shelter to the impoverished. The truth is, nobody cares about your bank account. When you are on your deathbed you cannot tell the doctor to help you put millions of dollars in the grave with you. As that is foolish and unreasonable. No matter what you believe in, your riches cannot be transferred into an after-death account. So why do we hoard? Why do we save for a rainy day? Our possessions, why do we value them more than ourselves? Well, we can go on a positive route first. In an emergency, in a crisis, it is smart to have some money set aside in case anything happens. Johnny broke his elbow doing this, or Isabel needs surgery. In those situations, it makes sense. We value our possessions because of our fear of them being taken away. Because we cannot take our money to the grave, that should take the pressure off. People who hoard money tend to operate on a scarcity mindset. This is the opposite of abundance. You have an obsession with the things you lack. Naturally, we want what we cannot have. As a result, we look to satisfy our egos. We believe that we will be happy if we had these possessions. An abundance mindset will push you to accomplish as much as you can. People save money and hoard money. What is the difference? When people hoard money, they have a fear of being broke. They do not want to be separated from their friends and family so they try to accumulate as much money as possible. Saving money has a purpose. This could be a teen saving up for a new car or a married couple saving for retirement. Saving is holding the money to spend it once you reach a certain amount. Hoarding is holding the money and never spending it. If you have the fear of going broke, then there of some things that you can do right now to free yourself. Tracking your income and expenses is the classic move. Perhaps it was harder for you before the age of technology began. Everyone likes to be rewarded for their hard work, and it feels nice to reward yourself every so often. It does not matter where you work. Anybody can learn financial literacy. So start small. For example, you could take your monthly income, track your expenses, then see what you can spend or save. Doing this will help you create a budget. You need to spend less on your stomach so that you have more to invest later. So you might set a budget of only ten dollars, five dollars, or you can bring your lunch to work. This is just a small part of your day. Think about the other goods or services you are spending too much money on. We like the feeling of buying and consuming everything that looks or tastes good. After a while, when the rush fades, we get what is called buyer's remorse. This is the regret you feel after making a purchase. I have experienced this when buying shoes and clothes. Yes, they were new. They did look good to me. I have flexed them. But what comes after that? Nothing. Within weeks or months, there will be a newer shoe, a newer piece of clothing. Like addiction, we convince ourselves that we deserve it. We deserve to flash our jewelry because we are in a different tax bracket. Why should I be humble if no one believed in me? So we buy items with little to no return on investments. Our possessions crowd our homes so guests can see that we have it all together. We hide our insecurities in what we wear, where we travel, and what we drive. When money starts to become your main focus, your main goal is to get more and more; it is excessive. When you put money in front of your family, friends, or those that have helped you along the way, you are blocking future blessings. You are denying future opportunities to make your community a better place. If you do not want to start there, then examine your family tree. How did you get there? How did people before you get there? You are not entitled to anything. Privilege can be stripped away at any moment. Money can be lost, stolen, or spent within one day. Do not operate out of fear, operate out of knowledge. The advice I will give to you is this, it is simple yet ignored. To save more, cut expenses. For individuals that are hoarding, look to invest in something you believe in. Every investor is looking to get a great return on investment. If you are advanced, then maybe you hold onto your shares, and plan according to the market. The scarcity mindset comes from the fear of being broke. If you do not hold onto this resource, then you can lose it, and then there is no way you can get it again. This is a lie. Think about the amount of money you want. Keep this to yourself. Now, why do you want that amount of money? Maybe you want to be the first millionaire in your family. It is possible that you just want to move your family out of the poor housing they currently live in. Perhaps it is because you want to enjoy life without worrying about the price tags. If your goal is to impress your friends and all the people who did not support you in the beginning, you will still feel empty. I have experienced this. You accomplished that goal, great. People are still going to criticize you no matter what. This portion about money has been focused on the individual; you. I want you to switch your mind to the external. Who are some people in your life that need real assistance? Is there someone that is drawing in debt or medical expenses? Could you contribute to their future well-being? I ask these questions to help you check in with yourself. Everyone grows up to have a moral compass. Depending on the situation, we adjust based on our values. Think about those that have blessed you financially and how that made you feel. As much as we like to serve ourselves, serving others is a different feeling. Leading others with the heart of a servant is powerful. When we are put in a position of power, we like to maintain it. In elementary school, maybe your teacher determined who was the line leader. It sounds silly, right? Usually, lines are in alphabetical order, but every once in a while, the teacher would switch it up. As the line leader, you are responsible for everyone behind you. Maybe you stopped at every intersection to wait for other classes to pass by. If you are currently an elementary teacher, a class that is quiet in the hallway gets rewarded. Switching back to the student, you are not completely in charge, but you can control the line. If you stop abruptly, then people run into each other. There was this phrase, "Ducktails and bubbles." Everyone had to put their hands behind their backs and close their mouths to be as quiet as possible. This was and still is an efficient way to avoid people touching each other or making obnoxious noises while passing classes. You have power. But if you abuse that power, then that position is often taken away from you. Then it is given to someone trustworthy. I use this example for an important reason. We need to recognize the levels of power from all walks of life.

Power is exciting. Being able to make decisions at the top is a great feeling. But what are the types of power? Which ones work more than others? Psychologists Bertram Raven and John French are known for their significant theories about power. They identified five types of power in leadership. Legitimate, reward, coercive, referent, and expert power are the five. Legitimate power comes from the position power given by an organization. Positional power stems from formal roles and titles, like CEO or supervisor. The teacher in the example has legitimate power given by the school and district. Reward power is based on the leader's ability to influence others with something valuable. A quiet class in the hallway gets rewarded. Maybe at the end of the day, everyone gets one piece of candy. This teacher also has coercive power. They can withhold rewards so their students comply. If you stay quiet during independent reading, you will receive a longer recess. But if you are loud and cause a distraction, you will not receive anything. Referent power comes from personal relationships. This person is seen as a role model. Other people are inspired and influenced when they hang around a person with this power. Lastly, expert power. This one is self-explanatory. When a person has gained skills and knowledge in a certain area, people can learn from them. If they have experience, maybe they can help the organization. An example of this would be someone fluent in a different language helping the organization. They can break that barrier and continue business with future partners. Ethically, all five of these types can be used to benefit the team. So what happens when leaders become power-hungry? We must be clear on the reasons why people starve for more power. This is different for everyone, as we have our own goals. Power is necessary. There will always be owners of businesses, leaders of subgroups, new employees, and those elected who have some power. In a perfect world, we hope for more individuals that seek power to inspire others. People that use their power to benefit others rather than themselves are influential. Maintaining that power takes discipline. Consequently, sometimes we look at power negatively. From what we have seen in the past, we highlight the destructive individuals. They were coercive and had evil intentions. It is smart to recognize these people because they are prime examples of what not to do. Understand that wanting more power is not bad. Working to get to a certain position with more freedom and decision-making is not terrible. Without power, nothing gets done. Personal power is based on charisma and personality. You would not have friends if you had no personal power. This is not something you are born with, but it is learned through shared experiences. They like playing the piano, you like playing the drums. You become good friends because you both play instruments. Years down the line, maybe you want to learn the piano. Who has the skills and knowledge to teach you? Your friend. They might not be world-renowned professionals but they do possess expert power. Perhaps we seek power to fulfill our egos. Deep down you know who you are. The strengths you have, you capitalize on. However, your weaknesses might be neglected because you enter into an unfamiliar space mentally. With that being said, low self-esteem can cause rage and obsession with being at the top. This blocks the ability to be mindful. As long as you can control others, you will not have to worry about being in a low position again. This is what individuals believe when the cravings hit. We glorify powerful individuals throughout history. Whether they did it ethically is up to you to decide. Think about a time when you felt powerless. A time when your heart felt like it was ripped out of your chest. When life hit you so hard that you lost the energy to get back up. Go to that place. What was going through your mind? Picture it. Now, look at where you are now. What have you done to get that power back? If you do not have it right now, what can you do to get there? Whatever organization you work for you have some power. In your friend groups, each individual has something that nobody else has. Did the event you visualized drive you to become the person you are today? Maybe you grew up in a household where you had no say in anything. I want you to judge yourself. Pay attention to the following signs of a power-hungry individual. If you are a manager or leader in your organization, this will apply to you. One sign is the lack of trust in your team. If you cannot trust your players, employees, and others under your watch, then you are less likely to have a stable relationship.When you only believe in your ways of operation, you close the door to new opportunities. The talent that you have within your organization is not utilized. The new ideas get left out. Nobody wants to work for an individual who wants complete control over everything. If you get jealous or angry when someone else is in charge, you might be power-hungry. Maybe you are the youngest or middle child and never got to be in charge when your parents left the house. So you always had to follow orders from someone else. After some time, you got tired of that. This is not your fault. You did not choose to be the youngest. I understand that. But leaders can project their insecurities on their subordinates. This can create a toxic environment. Members of the organization might feel the need to try harder to win over the boss. Now everyone is competing for power and productivity going down. Another symptom of this problem is degrading people who have different beliefs. If you are not willing to accept others because they do not think the way you do, then you are in for a life of loneliness. You will not get along with everyone you meet. This is okay. What if the person you are dealing with has some data that a group of people wants? This is information power. If they had a relationship with an influential person, maybe it would benefit you to respect them. This is connection power. You can help these people, and build a relationship that strengthens both parties. So if you are a power-hungry individual, what can you do to stop that behavior? First, you need to take ownership. No matter what your role is, the organization is not where it needs to be. If you are the manager, it is best to accept responsibility. Look at what happened on your watch. Check on the employees and other members that are lacking. See how you should approach the process of getting them on board. When you develop your team and focus on progress, the culture changes. A great leader can turn a horrible environment into a thriving workplace. They do not accomplish it on their own. The team also contributes. We see how much influence one person can have on social media. Our time is sometimes spent following what others are doing even if it is unethical. If they got to the top by manipulating people, then we want to manipulate them too. The actions you take will catch up to you. Why do we like power? Great moves are made when people have them. This is attractive. There is a bit more freedom than someone who is always second or third in command. On the whole, power is not evil. However, when used incorrectly to fulfill bad intentions it becomes evil. In another way, it can be used to change the world. A people-first attitude can solve several problems. When a person reaches the top and leads others by example or by teaching, it is inspiring. Those that have learned from that person have hope. In the future when they are leaders in the world, they will want to teach others. The cycle continues and builds generations of effective leaders and followers. Sex, money, and power. Three words with negative connotations. These are parts of our lives. When we abuse what we have, it can be lost. Sex is everywhere because it sells. We like to be seduced by short commercials about products we use daily. For consumers to buy the company needs to grab their attention, submit a call to action, and hope for the best. Sexual content is accessible from every social media app and there are websites dedicated to it. Financially, we say we want to make more money so we can buy luxuries to put on display. We want to hide behind our bank accounts so people do not know the real us. The comparisons are made to people we admire because their net worth is seven figures or above. We find ourselves depressed because we worry about money. In our lives throughout the week, we work for someone else. Our desire for power is through the roof and we are famished. The distractions overflow our minds. We question our purpose. The people we surround ourselves with are doing better, but why? Envy starts to set in. The race to the top has not started or ended. With every new individual chasing the high of being first, the finish line moves further. The destructive activities that involve sex, money, and power might seem free, but they cost you your time and energy. When left unchecked, they cost you your life. Make your own choices, but know that there is a consequence. A lifestyle that drains you should not be accepted. You will face challenges, that is a guarantee. We have all made mistakes that we knew could have been avoided. Do not beat yourself up. Forgive yourself. Have hope. You do not have to conform to all the things this world has to offer. Now is the perfect time to create, grow, and inspire others to grow with you. Use your resources wisely. You will thank yourself later.

CHAPTER 11

FAITH

Confidence can transform your life. This comes from believing in what you do consistently. When you wake up and turn on the lights, you trust that your electricity is working. When you turn on the shower in the bathroom, you believe that water will come out. On a road trip to a new place, you trust that your digital maps will give you the fastest route. Whatever it is, we all have faith in something. This could be our belief in God, other religions, or people. In some cases, we do not need proof to believe. Nowadays, it can be hard to find purpose in a world that causes us to suppress our dreams and think logically. Contrary to popular belief, you have a purpose. You are not living today by accident. The chances of being born are 1 in 400 trillion. Think about that for a second. You had a higher chance of not existing at this moment. If anyone has told you that you do not matter, then they do not deserve to be in your life. Respectfully, I want you to stop believing you are worthless. There are enough outlets telling everybody that same lie each day. This should comfort you. Everyone around is there for a reason. Look at the activities you enjoy doing. Early in life, some of us know our passions, others might need to be brought out. With that being said, do not ignore your passions. If you do, you will be working your whole life in a miserable state. Now, there is work to be done so that you can live your dream. There is more to life than being human. The communities surrounding spirituality are growing. Spirituality itself is the quality of being spiritual. With this, there is a belief in something; a higher power. Whatever that looks like for you or people you know. We like to feel worthy. Our time is spent searching in the wrong places and right places. I was born and raised in a Christian home. Being in the church was instilled in me early. The best friends I have today, I met in church. In third grade, I accepted Jesus into my heart. This happened one night in the middle of the school year. I prayed, confessed my sins, repented, and accepted. In the same year, 2011, I got baptized. If you are familiar with baptism, in Christianity it is an outward expression of an inward commitment. This was the part in my story that built my character. Everyone loves good character development. Having God in my life grew my confidence. I built new relationships with people and invited friends to church. I had extra support twice a week. As I grew older, Wednesdays were for deeper conversations. In middle school, you are living crucial years of life. Your growth is based on the friends you make and the work you put in. By high school, you sort of know who your circle is. You begin to stick by those people. But maybe it is the opposite. Maybe you found your true friends in high school and got rid of the ones that dragged you down. In church, I got used to sudden change. The turnover rate for pastors in my first eighteen years in the church was high. It was hard to commit to one pastor when they would leave in two to three years. I had three different youth pastors before middle school. After a couple of years, three pastors went through our young adult ministry. Being a follower made me a better leader on my teams. In every sport I played, I lead by example. As I became more comfortable, I got vocal. Through reading the Bible, I learned how to control my emotions. When I played basketball, I used to foul out most of the games and get at least one technical foul. I was taught to do everything like I was doing it for the Lord. The apostle Paul wrote the book of Colossians after a visit with the evangelist of the church in Colossae, named Ephesus. One verse from this book that has stuck with me recently is Colossians 3:17(NLT), "And whatever you do or say, do it as a representative of the Lord Jesus, giving thanks through him to God the Father." No matter what I do, I must give thanks to God. He is the one that gives me energy throughout the day. This helps me keep my faith, even in trying times. Studying the Bible is a continuous process.

But I have a few verses that have stuck with me for years. Being able to go to church twice a week forced me to be in the community. I was not the only one trying to improve. Everyone had their baggage. But I had pastors and friends to hold me accountable. I did the same for them. Every Sunday people who walked into the sanctuary would be greeted by an usher and then given a paper for the sermon. This was a long sheet of paper with the verses and main points of the sermon on it. On the back were announcements and online giving opportunities. I started taking notes on this page consistently in high school. In middle school, I would try to remember instead of writing. Sometimes, I would make a verse on my wallpaper so I would not forget it. The verses that I learned years ago, still apply to my life today. When they come up, I know that it is God telling me something. I am big on purpose. If I can enjoy doing the things I am supposed to do in this life, then I will be satisfied. On my walk with God, the content I consumed surrounded him. In my attempts to feed myself positive energy, I would follow more pastors. In addition to this, I did tons of reading plans on the Bible app. The app tracks how many days the user visits, and it gives the user a streak. Along with this are total weeks on the app. One mistake I made with this was doing the plans just to get the highest streak and not retain the information. I would click through the plans and verses. On the days when I was angry at God or discouraged in my situation, I kept seeing and hearing this one verse. In the book of Joshua chapter one, verse nine; "This is my command - be strong and courageous! Do not be afraid or discouraged. For the Lord, your God is with you wherever you go." Now when I was first introduced to this verse, I was furious. I had questions for God. At the time, it felt like everywhere I went, he was not there. But he was. I saw how corrupt the world was and felt like I was powerless. How would I get rid of those feeling when it felt like God was nowhere near me? Truthfully, I was ignoring him. Every time I passed on reading the Bible, there was an opportunity to get closer to God. The instinct when we face adversity and resistance is to flee. We do not like discomfort so we do everything we can to live comfortably. Having faith in anything can help you grow in discomfort. When you find meaning in life, you have to drive. If you have ever been around someone ambitious, you know that they have high energy. They are fun to be around and you want to stay around them. When your circle is full of ambitious people, you are almost forced to level up. You get that feeling inside that helps you become more self-aware. Once you get that energy, you take action. Now that you have found your purpose, you believe in yourself. The moves you make are different. You start to align everything you do to reach that one goal that is on your mind. Even if you work a 9-5, that time in between the next shift, you are chasing your dream. When you look too far into the future, you might raise your anxiety levels. Imagining the worse scenarios in your head can keep you in the same place. One verse that relates to anxiety comes from the book of Philippians. "Do not be anxious about anything, but in every situation by prayer and petition, with thanksgiving, present your requests to God. And the peace of God, which transcends all understanding will guard your hearts and your minds in Christ Jesus" - Philippians 4:6-7(NIV). In times when I was in my head, I would pray. Some of the prayers were selfish but I had the right intentions. Most of it was me telling God I needed to be healed as soon as possible. It took me years to realize that my plans are not final. According to the Bible, God has a pleasing and perfect will for my life and yours. This was and still can be hard to understand. When we do everything right in the pursuit of what we want and still end up failing, it is heartbreaking. You cannot control every circumstance. God gave us free will to go after what we want, moral and immoral. Yet, when we fall short, then turn to Him, he welcomes us with open arms. He is always there even if you do not believe him. No matter how far you have gone, God will accept you right where you are. When you accept Jesus into your heart and start going to church, the results you desire are not automatic. You are not immune to the evils of this world. What you have is someone to talk to, at any time of the day or night. Being involved in the church allows you to serve others by using your gifts. If you enjoy playing the drums or violin, you could be on the worship team. Maybe the choir needs an extra voice, that could be you. For those who want to invest in future generations, volunteering in the ministries for toddlers and children is essential. If you are into production and technology, you can be behind the scenes with the lights and cameras. Through the church of other places, you can build relationships that thrive for years. What do most people look for in relationships? What should be a non-negotiable when it comes to searching for a partner? Loyalty. The person who sticks with you through thick and thin is reliable. The friends who are loyal to you most likely have your trust.

Trustworthiness is invaluable. Sometimes we go through life having faith in things and people that do not benefit us. I am not saying you should only let people in that can benefit you without contributing to their success, no. However, having individuals around you that you trust is important. They are there to hold you accountable and you continue to learn from them. As the years go by, you can build an impenetrable circle. What does that mean? Well, the world today is focused on the individual. When we look at professional sports and look at the best teams, we like to talk about the individual. The team that is highly ranked may have an unstoppable defense, but the coverage is focused on the quarterback. A company may have influential employees that have come up with the best ideas, but the CEO gets the credit. So the world becomes faithful to that one player on the team, or the company. But there is a positive part to this. A player with extraordinary talent and commitment is trusted. The coaches trust this person. On a professional team, the front office trusts this person. When the game is on the line and the team is down two, the ball is in the hands of this player. When it is fourth and inches, the player is ready to get the first down. When the company had a bad quarter or year, everyone looks to the leader to adjust. They have faith in this person. Why? Somewhere along the way, they have proven themselves worthy. In crunch time, they delivered. They turned a dark cloud of negativity into a bright day of productivity. Now whenever that dark cloud comes back, they are ready. So the automatic response is to turn to them. Think about who you have faith in. Clearly, in your eyes, this person is trustworthy. Maybe they have led you to become a better person. They might be a mentor that helped you close a deal or get the job you wanted. Maybe it is a parent. Every time you felt down, they were there to keep you calm. The world today is testing your faith, whether you are religious or not. When you start to tell the people close to you what you are trying to do in this life, you will receive hate. The life you desire may require sacrifice. Maybe you need to disappear for a few months to focus on yourself. As a result, you lose friends. The people that trusted you to stay on their level are envious. Maybe you stay on this continuous path of holistic self-improvement, and to some, you are at the top. The people that left you back then, are here now. Picture yourself running a marathon. They were there in the beginning, but on mile six, year six; they left. But twenty miles later, you see them at the finish line. They are waiting for you at the finish line so they can benefit. Through the years they lost their faith, they did not trust you. When you left the group, they stayed. You saw their potential back then and they failed to realize it. You had faith in your future self. So you took the risks. Unfortunately, we are being taught to put our faith in destructive activities. At some point, maybe in childhood or through our years of young adulthood, we are exposed to these activities. Drugs, sex, pornography, alcohol, nicotine, and laziness. So what happens to a person after relying on these things? They get stuck in their ways. The earlier you start a destructive habit, the harder it gets to quit as you age. A person who is chained to these habits has no faith in their future self. They only hang around people at this level and want nothing more for themselves. Each day is an opportunity to grow, but they waste their time. But there is another side to this. Besides religion, there are great things to put your faith in. A leader who is honest and effective should be trusted. The diet plan that you have set up for yourself is something you should trust. The trainer that gets in your head, the lifting partner that pushes you to do one more rep, should be trusted. Being a Christian pushed me outside of my comfort zone, especially when I wanted to stay comfortable. Put yourself in this situation. A person on a journey of improvement is often pushed outside of their comfort zone. This is common for everyone making an effort. You need people who challenge you. The accountability keeps you faithful. When I receive an invite to go through a Bible plan with someone, I have that accountability. On the Bible app, it tells you when you are behind or on track when reading a plan. You can just check the boxes and skip through without receiving the message. But what does this do? If you have no direction before your day starts, then you stay in the same place or end up somewhere you do not want to be. I have learned how to keep the faith. When I pray, I thank God for everything in my life, no matter how small. When I connect to Him each day, I do not have to be anxious. I do not have to be afraid of the future because of that connection. Luckily, I have been surrounded by faithful people. Everyone in my family was raised in the church. Every time I would visit my grandparents in Junction City, Kansas on a weekend, we would go to church. Their church was welcoming and it felt like a second home. I know that this is not the same for many people. Maybe you avoid trusting new people in your life because of your childhood. People that were supposed to take care of you might have neglected you. Maybe they left. You might have been raised in an abusive household. Watching your parents fight regularly changed you. Whatever the case may be, you turned to something or someone. I can never fully understand your situation. Living in the environment I described makes it harder to trust anyone who seems promising. So how is trust built? As someone who has trust issues, how do you overcome them? Unlike sudden change, you want to be gradual. You want to ease into trusting someone. We have all blindly followed someone only to be let down shortly after. The key difference between trust and a lack of it is communication. Through honest conversation, intentions can be made clear. Part of this requires some vulnerability. I remember being in a youth group when I was in middle school. The ministry was called 212 because in the church it was in room 212. The true meaning was that 212 degrees Fahrenheit is the degree of change. Water boils at this temperature. In the church, I was taught to be on fire for God. A lukewarm follower has one foot in and one out. Nothing gets done. There is no progress. The opportunities to be fully bought in are there. This is a gradual process. The water in the bowl does not start boiling immediately. Heat must be added. The heat is the uncomfortable conversations. A person strong enough to share their hurts deserves your respect. They trust you with the information they share. Without communication, we start to create unrealistic expectations of partners, friends, and family. When your expectations are not addressed, you will be unfulfilled. The same goes, from the perspective of the other side. Now, plenty of people get confused about control and trust. Control is an elementary-level word. To exercise control, an individual uses tactics to get what they want. Using coercion and rewards are just a couple that is used. A threat of force is unhealthy in any relationship. Especially when things get physical. When the boundaries are set in the beginning, the intentions are clear, and both parties know what to expect. Trust is simply relying on another person based on what they do when you are there and when no one is watching. You will learn to see right through them when they are being dishonest. At the same time, they are counting on you to be the strong person they know you can be. When you spend time away from this person, you will never know exactly what they are doing all the time. There is nothing wrong with this. You cannot control every aspect, and if you try, you are destroying that person psychologically. When you cannot trust someone, it causes them to question you. Trust needs to be at the top of your priority list in your relationship. I am no expert, but this should be the foundation. Without a solid foundation, the house crumbles and every storm consumes it. You do not have to open up to every person you meet. But being completely closed off might not yield the results you want. What is your faith in? Have you been following the wrong people? I want you to think about the people you put your trust in. You know all the good qualities you look for. It is quite a common list if you ask a handful of people. But what are the bad qualities? What should you look for if you think a person is unfaithful? The obvious sign is a lack of commitment. You can tell when a person is deficient in this area. When it is time to commit, this person leaves or neglects others. When commitment is gone, the love goes with it. How could you love someone you are not committed to? They will either give you more love and stay with you or recognize you and then leave. Maybe they came from a rough environment that did not show them, love, at an early age. The people who were supposed to raise them with love might have abused them. So the only way they can operate is out of anger. How do you deal with these people? They keep their distance, so it is hard to get close. It seems like it would take a miracle for them to open up. If they do not feel confident when talking to you, ask yourself why. Maybe you came off too strong and you have not earned their trust. This is not all your fault. You are not responsible. But it is up to you to create a bond if you care about this person. If you see that they are not fit for you, or you for them, then you can spend less time with them. Being patient with this person might mean putting your pride to the side. Dealing with difficult people is not fun. It is not supposed to be. Most people have stronger bonds with people through shared experiences. You grow together. The needs are met and you receive peace of mind. The relationship is secure and your partner feels protected. As long as you keep each other accountable, problems that come up will be solved. At the very least, you learn. Through years of having different coaches, teachers, and mentors, I have been able to put my trust in efficient leaders. I have seen how they act under pressure and when everything is going fine. The common quality I see is constant progress. They do not get stuck in one way of thinking and hold onto it. They build off their beliefs by strengthening them. When the methods work, they look for ways to make them better. If something is not working, they adjust. The people they serve, players and students; react to the change. There will be some support and resistance, this is natural. I want you to be able to discern. I want you to separate the strong relationships from the weak ones. If you are being built up and pushed to be your greatest, then keep going. If you are being neglected, and the person is tearing you down, then leave. I know that is easier said than done if you have been with this person or group for years. Some resources will help you free yourself. Believe that you do not have to stay in your situation. There is a way out. In my life, I have had destructive friends. Everything they did go against my values. To leave them was hard, but when I did, the weight off my shoulders was lifted. I did not have to put on a different personality around them. I did not have to meet their standards. God allowed these people to be in my life so that I could learn from them. You will meet excellent examples and horrible examples of people. You can learn from both. I did. Eventually, what was for me came to me. What was not for me showed me, and I recognized it based on my intuition. There was a direct correlation between my well-being and how close I got to God. When I faced some tough decisions, as we all will sooner or later, I found it harder to panic. Hebrew 13:8 (NIV) says, "Jesus Christ is the same yesterday and today and forever." I applied this verse in times when God felt distant. There were many instances where I was selfish and let my ego drive me. We have all done this. The lack of respect I had for myself made me depressed. I was not happy with what was happening to me. Sometimes I would talk to God angrily, and go to bed in a bad mood. Yes, I was raised in the church. I was around plenty of people that guided me. But if I did not believe in myself, in my growth, then I would get nothing out of it. The same is true for you. Believing in something changes your behavior. You start to grow in your faith. The next step is believing in yourself. No matter what you have been told by others, you are worthy. Like I said before, you had a higher chance of not being born. To go through life aimlessly is disrespectful to your future self. When you go after what you want, there will be people that support you. Do not believe the lie that absolutely no one will be with you. You have value as a human being. The goals you have are not in your mind for no reason. In most action movies, the hero receives a call to action. Maybe this is in the form of a disaster or something that directly affects their way of living. What was once comfortable is now uncomfortable. It takes faith to step into a season of uncertainty. The one move you need to make might change your life for the better. Believing in yourself helps you achieve those goals. You start to seek the help you need to level up. When you reach the top of one mountain, you see dozens of mountains to conquer. Your brain starts to produce ideas that would not be cultivated before. In your mind, you paint a picture of the look and feel of success. I have said before how important visualization is. People with a vision tend to do everything in their power to make it a reality. Others sit on the couch, uninspired, and put their lives on cruise control. Life has no speed limit. You can go as slow or as fast as you can. Sometimes it is a slow process and you need to build up speed. Jumping into it and learning as you go might be the best way. You have been gifted with abilities that can take you far. If you had something powerful in a box that can be shared with the world, it would be hard to hide it. When you bring that box out, great things happen. Why would you keep this box to yourself? After some time, you would get the urge to share it. So why not start now? While yesterday was the best time to start, today can be that day. Take a leap of faith for yourself. Acknowledge the emotions that have carried you to this point. Turn your words and thoughts into action. Watch what happens. Have faith.

CHAPTER 12

IMPOSTOR SYNDROME

We all know what an imposter is. They are deceitful. When we watch tv shows and hear the characters say, "impostor!" we know the person is a fraud. A person with this label pretends to be someone else for personal gain. They are usually the characters we root against. At least villains are true to themselves. Most villains we see just want more power. Sometimes they do not want to be anyone else. They know what they want. When the word fraud gets thrown around in the media, it means that this person is not who they say they are. Around colleagues or other important people, they put on a show. They act like they have it all together, and when the road gets bumpy, their true colors show. This is seen in cases that involve embezzlement, defamation, and other offenses. A syndrome is a characteristic. It might create a disorder, something that affects social life. Multiple symptoms add up and the result is a syndrome. These are two different words that we hear often. But what do they have to do with each other? They have their definitions. What happens when you put them together? What is this thing called impostor syndrome? How does it change your outlook on life? Does everyone suffer from this? If you are not familiar with this concept, it is natural to have similar questions. Impostor syndrome is essentially self-doubt through accomplishments. This is setting extremely high standards for yourself. It is dissatisfaction when you reach a goal. Someone with impostor syndrome believes that they do not deserve the success they have accumulated. They feel like a fraud. As a result, they feel like they do not belong. The root cause of impostor syndrome is perfectionism. A perfectionist does not submit any work that is not flawless in their eyes. They believe people will not accept them. Fear of judgment is on their mind at all times. If their work does not meet their standards, they do nothing. Small problems and setbacks make this person depressed. They feel worthless if their creation is imperfect. Picture a child drawing a picture of a house, some trees, the Sun, and birds. After drawing one picture, they look at it and crumple it up. Why? It is not good enough. They start over. The next drawing is hideous. So they crumple it up and throw it away. An hour passes. After throwing away twenty sheets of paper, they finally get one right. Soon after, they feel like the other ones were better. Their teacher compliments them, but they avoid the praise. One person saw the drawing, but the child does not want to share it with anyone else. They are afraid of what others will say. There is a fear of rejection here. We all have experienced some form of imposter syndrome There were times when I was a perfectionist. When I first started journaling on July 1, 2021, I wanted to make the journal perfect. Another time was when I started writing this book. Questions were on my mind. Should I start? What will my friends say? I am not a well-known author so who am I to share this message? I could have easily stopped writing because it was not perfect. If you are a perfectionist, maybe your parents had unrealistic expectations of you. Due to these expectations, the standards of the world caught your attention. I also feared rejection. This increases the feelings of loneliness. Being rejected drove me crazy. But it also drove me to be my version of the best. I used to suppress feelings and exert the built-up energy through lifting and running. When I finished a workout, the feelings would come back. This was a form of escapism. In a way that I thought was helping me, some of it was hurting me. How do you defeat this? Learn your lesson. You will continue to be taught the same lesson until you fully learn from it and move on. Do not move on for others. Move on for yourself; your mental health. Face your fear. If you are afraid of being rejected, then talk to more people. If you are introverted, even better. You now have a challenge. It is up to you. Fear of rejection can block future success and relationships.

Understand that whatever you do in life big or small, people will accept you and reject you. If you buy a black car, people will say the red version looks better. If you make six figures, people will wonder why you are not making seven. On the other side, something that you think is small can make a big impact on someone. Smiling at a stranger, asking them how they are doing; a small task. But this can make both you and the stranger feel good, even if it is for a few minutes. People will have their opinions about everything. You will go insane trying to please everybody. Going back to the perfectionist qualities. This is only one of five types of impostors. How do you deal with the perfectionist? People that aim to get a 100% on a test and end up getting a 97% that are disappointed are like this. They degrade themselves. You help them by highlighting their commitment. This person loves their work and they stop at nothing to do their best. But if they continue to discredit their success, it can make them a liability to the team. They might need you to remind them that their work is acceptable. The next type is the expert. The expert believes in accumulating enough knowledge to know anything about everything. This person does not feel qualified. So they do their research, read more, and watch more. The problem is they want to know everything. When they are challenged with a question, they want to know the answer. If they do not have the answer then they are discouraged. They fear being the one that does not know the answer. A person who is always gaining knowledge can be helpful in the future. But you must tell them that they will not have an answer for every question thrown at them. Knowing everything is impossible. It is one certainty that the expert in your life needs to accept. I had the problem of trying to be an expert when I started lifting. Before I went to the gym, I would look up workouts. I would study the different movements and techniques. I did this because I was afraid of embarrassing myself in front of other gym members. When my friends saw what I was doing they would question me. I always wanted to have the answer. I wanted to be that person that they turned to when they had fitness questions. Sometimes I was learning in the process of teaching them. In my free time, I kept watching videos and reading articles about what the best workout is. Everyone has their favorite workout, so I was bombarded with many opinions. I put on some muscle, I looked like I knew what I was doing. By the end of every workout, I wanted to be completely exhausted. Each time I walked through those doors, I wanted to leave everything out there. When I started seeing results, it was harder to accept criticism. After lower back pain, and muscle cramps, I finally accepted the advice from people stronger than me. I was no expert, I was just experienced. There is a difference. This leads to the next type, the soloist. Keyword solo. I would say that I had soloist tendencies early in life. A soloist does not ask for help. They see themselves as a fraud if they get assistance from someone else. If they got help on a presentation from an outside source and get praised for it, they deflect the praise onto the person that helped. For them, nothing counts unless they do it on their own. This is the girl making pancakes alone when her mother swoops in to flip them. In her mind, it does not count. So when her dad asks if she did it by herself, she replies "mommy helped me." Simple things like that. It is the teenager getting a spot from the biggest guy in the gym. He is bench pressing twice his weight but the bar starts to go down after the second rep. His spotter lifts it for him and says, "three" loudly. He tells him good job, but the teenager says, "I only did two by myself." While this is true, there is nothing wrong with receiving extra help. We have been conditioned to see "self-made" individuals in the media and envy them. Self-made is often thrown around. This person received media attention, committed employees, and numerous resources to get to where they are. A soloist moves into a house on their own. They carry all the heavy boxes and do not contact anyone to help. Asking someone who has gone through the process is not begging. It is not a form of weakness. Having the right resources can change your life. But we believe it does not work because we are afraid. Moving into a house is faster with four people than it is with one. You do not have to prove yourself by always flying solo. A person who respects themselves and their future will ask. If you want to eat, you have to open your mouth. To get a spotter, you have to ask. When learning a new skill, you better be asking for help. This is not a suggestion. If you want to be great, you will. The fourth type is superhuman. This is a common one among young adults. For adults, being this type of impostor puts even more stress on their lives. Think about your favorite superhero. In the movies, they seem to be everywhere at once. Their life outside of being this hero is balanced. They are the best in every area of their lives. When we sit at home or in a theater, we cannot help but put ourselves in their shoes. We compare our real lives to fictional ones. Why am I great in the office, but my marriage is failing? Why is my marriage going smoothly, but my work is not appreciated? Do I even deserve to be here if I am not the best at what I do? A superhuman wants to be the best in every area of their life. They want to be the best at work, at home, and out in public. When you see them post on social media, you can tell they want you to know how great life is. Now, there is nothing wrong with wanting to be the best. If you are not hungry, then you stay average.But this person goes the distance when it comes to being superior. This person overloads themselves with work. They cover up their insecurities because they want to do it all. What an amazing story it would be to have the label, best husband, wife, teacher, and volunteer. When people describe the superhuman, they picture a workaholic that seems to have it all figured out. How do they do it? They are excelling at everything and never stop. It is almost annoying to be around this person because of this. The downside is, that this person feeds off external validation. If other people do not like them, then they do not like themselves. So they strive to keep pushing and force their way into success. Instead of being fulfilled, they continue. This can go on for a while and once something bad happens, they shut down. They get passed up. How could this happen? Their mentality was off from the beginning. Unfortunately, they suffer from burnout. They are exhausted. You can still guide this person on a better path. Failure is inevitable. It is certain. They might need to pull back a little bit. You can drive a car at 100 miles per hour all you want, but sooner or later, you are going to need gas. Maybe new tires, and more. This person needs to learn how to accept who they are. They need to know that they cannot do it all. Saying no to certain activities is important for someone that wants to stop being superhuman. The last type is the 'natural genius'. Similar to perfectionists, they want to be right. More specifically, they want to be perfect the first time. They have a fixed mindset. In their mind, they believe everyone who is a great leader was born that way. Every artist was born with a moving voice. This is not true. Every skill someone has is amplified through experience. If you never played baseball in your life, you cannot expect to lead the MLB in home runs. Our favorite artists and players reached that level by working harder than most. They make it look easy. When natural geniuses find it hard to complete a new task, they stop believing. Since they are not going through the work with absolute ease, they feel inadequate. To change this person, they need to first change their mindset. A fixed mindset will not benefit them later in life. When they switch that to a growth mindset, they can be confident in their work. In the past, the initial thought would be they were not born for this. They will disqualify themselves. But after intervention and soul searching, the belief is that they can accomplish anything they work for. Through learning and asking for help, they can reach that desired level. Have you ever been around someone that seems to be great at everything they try? It might spark some jealousy within you. Just like the superhuman tendencies, whatever they touch makes them successful. Why do you feel jealous? There is something that they have that you lack. Too many people believe that they cannot learn. But they can. Today, there are thousands of resources to learn anything. Not everything you try will come easy. The first time you play the piano, make art, or create content does not have to be perfect. The fact that you started is good. This is the first step. Be a lifelong student. When you reach that higher level; teach others if you can. You are always progressing. Improvement should be a priority, but not to the point of burnout. When I look at my achievements, I remember times when I acted like all five types. As a child, I was more of a perfectionist and soloist. In middle school, I behaved like a natural genius. My mindset was fixed at the time. In high school, I wanted to be an expert and superhuman. We have all experienced this. I have defined the five types. But this does no good if you do not know how to overcome your struggles. The process of overcoming this may sound simple, but if you have been deeply rooted in these behaviors, it will take time. First, you need to remove some of the pressure that you put on yourself. This is the hardest for me. Maybe your fear is never amounting to anything, so you keep yourself busy. If you are like me, then you apply more pressure on yourself than anyone ever could. This is will stop you in your tracks when left unchecked. Next, you need to identify your habits. Your thought patterns are essential too. Negative self-talk equals negative results. In a world of criticism, be kind to yourself. While criticism can force you to be better, too much of that from your inner voice can hurt you. Think about what you want to get done. Set smart goals. Specific, measurable, attainable, relevant, and time-based. I am sure you are familiar with this, but it does not hurt to go through this process again. Make sure to check yourself when you feel like procrastinating. Delaying the work is easy. Saying you will do it the next day turns into the next week, then a month. After a year of procrastination, you will be in the same place complaining about the same things. You should not want this. If you have ever been to a track meet or remember racing your friends on the playground, you know that there is always one that looks at others. When you run next to them, you feel like they are staring at you and not the finish line. If you were this person, then you would look at others before the race ended. Just a peak. Right? You wanted to see how they ran so that you could catch up and beat them. You analyzed your opponents' strides then tried to match them and win. Usually, not all the time, but most of the time, the person that looks at others while running does not finish first. The ones who do look at others and win could have been faster. What you need to do is stop comparing yourself to others. This cannot be said enough. Most of our insecurities come from comparing ourselves to our favorite people. We try to follow in their footsteps and forget that success is not one size fits all. Instead of ending your day thinking about everything that did not work, think about what worked. When you lay your head on your pillow at the end of the day, you should be grateful for the wins. Taking the risks includes taking losses. Like a boxer, you need to take it to the chin and keep fighting. If you won more than you lost, accept the praise. Do not deflect it with a "yea, but" attitude. Of course, there will be some things you can improve upon, that is life. But do not sell yourself short. When you are too busy comparing and taking losses personally, you forget who you are. Know your worth. I mean sit down with yourself. If you need to, list your achievements. This will make you appreciate what you have been through to get where you are now. This activity should push you to go after more. Why stop at everything on the list? You should not be satisfied, but you can be grateful. The losses will pop into your head, but it took those losses to create that list. Once you realize that everything will not be perfect, you start to do more. I have one common question for you that you might have seen multiple times. What would you do if you knew you could not fail? What is that thing you have a burning passion for that you are afraid to capitalize on? There is something that you keep visualizing, that is keeping you up at night. What if you tried and did not fail? What if you could become that success story that inspires millions? Does this not brighten your day when thinking about it? I am not sure what goes through your mind. But when I imagine what I can accomplish without failing, I feel energized. While you cannot be perfect in everything you do, you can still be great. With this knowledge, you should have a reason to get out of bed. It might take one more move to put you in the new life your dream about. If you are good at what you do, embrace it. There is nothing wrong with being a skilled person. Through discipline and grit, you got to that point. You cannot deny results because it took work. Talk to someone close to you about your feelings. After a deep conversation or a quick one, you will find that these beliefs are limiting you. One of the main reasons why people suffer in silence is fear. It comes from a place in their mind where judgment and rejection collide. The individuals suffer alone because they feel alone. Imposter syndrome is something that most people face. You are not an outlier. With that in mind, you should talk more about it. We have irrational fears, it is okay. Continuing to act out because of these fears can paralyze you. While this has been discussed and researched for years, we fail to reach out in our circles. There were two times during high school when I felt like an imposter. One of them is the spring of my junior year. We had lost the state championship months before to an extremely disciplined team. I was a receiver during my first two years. As a junior, I played cornerback. The lack of intensity on defense was the main cause of us losing. Vision is 20/20 in hindsight. There were plenty of factors. So my head coach decided to bring on a new defensive coordinator. I remember being pulled aside after weights to talk to him. He looked at me and said, "I want you to be the leader of the defense. Are you ready?" My initial thought was why me? I had only played one year of the varsity on the defensive side of the ball. How could I be the one to lead this team? I am just a junior. Is there someone else that can do it instead? All of these questions I did not ask. When he told me this, I just said "Yes sir, I am ready." Coach Marinelli, the new defensive coach was excited. You would think that he had been at the school for years. I also got a new position coach, Coach Ike. Those two coaches did their best to change the culture of the defense. Our stats before they came were below average. As a defense in previous seasons, we would average twenty-eight allowed points per game. In playoff games, the number was higher. But after a summer of practicing, and bonding together as a team, we cut that number in half.

We would only average fourteen allowed points per game. Before my senior season, the team had to vote for captains. There would be three captains for the season, and one that would be picked every game. I was voted to be a captain during the whole season. When I found out I was going to be a captain, I felt like a fraud again. Playing in front of your family and friends is a blessing. But it can also bring feelings of self-doubt. At the beginning of the season, it was tough. During the first half of the season, at every coin toss, I felt out of place. But then we started winning by large margins. The game slowed down and I did not have to think as much. By the end of the regular season, our offense and defense broke school records. We went through the playoffs hungry. After beating teams from all around, we made it back to the state championship. We lost again. This was heartbreaking because some of my teammates would never lace up their cleats again. I left everything out there and I appreciate what I had to go through. With that being said, some of the pressure I put on myself was unreasonable. It took me some time to get over the loss. When you give it your all in what you are good at and fail, it hurts. I share this part of my story because it happens to everyone. We get to a position of authority and decline ourselves. When we experience the success we do not want to accept it. It is hard for us to believe that because we are not perfect individuals. The experts in their field who have done amazing things for the world have gone through a period of their life like this. Remember this, you are not a fraud. You have worked hard to get to this point. Celebrate the wins and learn from the losses. Persevere. Conquer.

CHAPTER 13

LEADERSHIP

L eadership is a widely studied topic. The earlier theories from the 1900s are less relevant today. But thankfully, some individuals kickstarted this study. The act of leading has been broken down into different types and the strategies used within those types. Motivating others to accomplish a shared goal takes work. The best teams and companies can have horrible leadership or effective leadership. Sometimes the process of reaching that shared goal took some sacrifice in unethical ways. Everywhere you look there are leaders. In school, you have your principal, administrators, then the teachers. Small businesses have owners, co-owners, and employees. Professional sports teams have owners, general managers, executives, and coaches. There is a chain of command. Why are we deficient in this topic? There are areas in our lives that lack leadership. In these situations, it can be hard to lead because we might be thrown into them without prior knowledge. In single-parent households, the child witnesses the leadership style of the one taking care of them. If they have to travel back and forth from different houses, they might have to adapt to the one taking care of them for a few days. Leadership, while it is a topic that has been studied for over a century, is not being taught to the majority. Some people never become leaders because they are scared. They have their mind set on never being this person that can teach others.

The truth is, with the right attitude and intentions, anyone can become a leader in any position. Just because you are an employee or not at the highest point does not mean you cannot work to be a leader. This world will always have followers, as they are essential to leaders. People might be led astray. Businesses fall apart, people lose jobs, or turn to dangerous habits. If they only know one way, then anything outside of that way is rejected. When this happens, nobody grows. They are fixed, solidified in their ways. Being a follower is easy today. On social media, we follow our favorite influencers, teams, and businesses we support. The catchphrases and amazing products motivate us to stay loyal. Their commercials persuade us to spend our money. When there is a face of the company or team, we remember them. If they tell us to buy something, we buy it. Think back to your childhood. There was that popular kid in your grade that influenced everyone on the playground. When they told their friends to jump, they jumped. If they needed someone to play with, all they had to do was ask or wave them over. From the outside, it makes sense. It was easy to follow this kid because most people were doing it. This person was the leader. Following is simply doing what the leaders ask of you. I am going to focus on followership. Depending on the state of the relationship between the follower and leader, the follower has a choice. In most cases, you have a choice. If the relationship is mutual and healthy, then this decision is not hard. However, when whatever the leader says goes and you do not have a voice, it can create some problems. One of the pioneers of followership Robert Kelley stated that "without followers, leadership is meaningless and leaders don't exist." Harvard public leadership professor Barbara Kellerman does an amazing job separating followers into five different categories. These types are based on the level of engagement. Isolates, bystanders, participants, activists, and diehards. Isolates are detached from the group. This person has the lowest level of engagement out of everyone. It might take some motivation and incentives to get them out of the isolated category. Next is the bystander. When you are witnessing a crime and do nothing, you are a bystander. On a team, if you witness success but do not contribute, you are a bystander. While the level of engagement is a bit higher than the isolate, you are simply an active observer. In sports leagues for children, when teams do not finish in the top three, sometimes they are given a participation trophy. Each kid gets one with their name and number on it. The participant is engaged but not completely bought in. They might give their time and do the bare minimum when it comes to working. Being active is important for your health. Similarly, an organization is healthier when the followers are activists. Then energy is much higher which produces higher commitment. Activists support their leaders and invest more than their time into the team. They might work against their leaders so they can replace them or dethrone them in the future. The highest level of engagement goes to the diehards. These are the people who paint their faces, pin their ears back, and get ready for war. They are willing to die for the cause they support. It is the worker that does not mind pulling all-nighters. This is the fan that shows up on the game day with all the gear and obnoxious accessories. At the highest engagement level, this person is extremely dedicated. Like the activist, the diehard can seek to destroy the leader as well. Years of following and being devoted might make them hungry to be the leader for once. Every move they make is based on their allegiance. Going back to Robert Kelley, created a model that separated followers based on their level of critical thinking and involvement. There are also five types, and they are ordered in quadrants, with one in the middle that exhibits all four styles. In the lower-left quadrant, there is the passive follower. They are low in critical thinking and involvement. As you might assume, they do not engage at all or think critically. This person is like wood in a lake; they drift along with no sense of direction. The conformist follower is found in the upper left quadrant. Although they are still low on critical thinking, their involvement is high. This is the person that agrees with everything. They say yes to everything. A conformist follower prefers to be told what to do. The effective follower is in the upper right quadrant. This is the optimal type you would want if you are the leader. Effective followers are high on involvement and critical thinking. They can lead without the leader. When the goals of the organization are made clear, they are motivated to reach them. The lower right quadrant is where the alienated followers are. They are low on involvement but their critical thinking is high. Alienated followers are not engaged but when the leaders want to go in another direction, they are skeptical. Sometimes they will voice their opinions, other times they will doubt the leader in silence. The last type of this model is the pragmatic follower. Depending on the situation, this person exhibits all four of the styles. They are on board with new ideas when they feel like it. In these situations, they can decide how involved they want to be. Their thought process is attached to their involvement too. A person can determine what type of follower they are based on their self-efficacy. There are online tests that you can take to see where you land on the model as well. Self-efficacy is the belief you have in your capabilities to produce at a certain level of performance. This has a major impact on your work ethic. Are you willing to support the team? Are you okay with putting everything on the line for your organization? The process of assigning responsibility and authority will be based on where you stand. We are all in different environments. In one place, you can be the passive or alienated follower. Especially if you are working in a new city, state, or country. Maybe you are familiar with your position as a follower, but you have the mindset of a leader. So you might fall between conformist and effective. As children, we were probably conformist followers during our first few years of school. Our teachers made us highly involved but we could not disagree because they were the leaders. This is not to say that you always agreed with what was taught. Some years pass and you start to become an effective follower, always raising your hand to answer questions. Or maybe you knew someone like this. If your parents enrolled you into every club under the sun, then you might have had some alienated tendencies. You never knew what you did not like before trying first. So there was that one activity that you were somewhat forced into that you disliked. After trying it, you decided to stop. You thought for a second that this was not for you, and you walked away. It takes courage to be an effective follower. Imagine how efficient a company could be with more than one of these people. How do you become an effective follower? One of the overlooked characteristics is listening. If you can take direction while thinking for yourself, you can become an effective follower. When there is no one clapping for you, you need to clap for yourself. You need to be able to motivate yourself because sometimes your leader cannot do it for you. Being a good teammate is contagious. When your colleagues see that you are energized and ready to help in any way, they will start to mimic you. Even when you fake enthusiasm, it can go a long way. On days when people are slacking, or not doing the work, you need to be the one to pick as many people up as possible. If you were a passive or conformist follower, you would want someone to give you a reason to reach the set goals. When you motivate others, you bring out the best in others. It drives them to become the teammate they need to be so everyone can win. When you are dealing with alienated followers, it is smart to collaborate. Listen to their ideas because those ideas might be the ones that push the organization in a winning direction. They are rarely involved, so they have time to think about the new ideas that they might be afraid to share. How confident are you in your abilities? Without some belief, it is hard to make progress. You cannot reach your full potential if you doubt yourself when trying new things. This goes back to perfectionism. Remove the idea that you will be perfect every time. It will not happen. However, you can use that to be great. Now that you know the different characteristics of each follower, it is time to lead. What type of leadership should you use? Which one is the most effective? We will begin with servant leadership. Larry C. Spears is an author who came up with the ten characteristics of a servant leader. He is the President and CEO of the Larry C. Spears Center for Servant Leadership, Inc. As a servant leader, you must ask yourself. How can others benefit? Being in this position is like planting trees knowing that you will never enjoy the shade. The first characteristic is listening. This is a simple skill that we learned in kindergarten, but it is still important today. Listening to understand and not respond is what makes people comfortable with speaking. Sometimes all a person needs is someone to listen to them. The next one is empathy, which is simply understanding the feelings of someone. This goes right next to the listening because when you show empathy, you temporarily remove your judgment. Everyone in the organization is different. They have different needs and process life in various ways. Healing and awareness are the third and fourth. In this age of technology, it is easier to hide your feelings through social media. When we are not seeing others physically, we starve for a real connection. A leader does not know the story of every follower. Maybe they are barely holding on emotionally, and need that extra boost. You never know what someone is going through. Treating the people around you well will keep the relationships solid. Servant leaders feel a responsibility to help broken people. They also have awareness, not only for themselves but for others. Being a self-aware individual, the servant leader knows their weaknesses and strengths. They use that power to make others aware. When you work on your weaknesses, you become stronger. There is no room for overcompensating. A leader that lacks awareness should not be followed. It is like they are steering a sinking ship with no plans to evacuate. Awareness puts the spotlight on problems internally and externally. Whether the leader wants to do something about it, it is up to them. If followers do not see that there is an issue, then nothing will get fixed. Having awareness helps the leader persuade. Persuasion is the next characteristic. Instead of forcing everyone to move by using force and threats, leaders bring a reason why followers should continue. Whatever the plans look like, while not set in stone, should be executed. What works can be optimized? This is where conceptualization comes into play. Servant leaders who think conceptually can see the bigger picture. They focus on what needs to be done within a year but also keep in mind what needs to be done in ten years. For the organization, they seek to scale the potential growth. This person needs to have a general idea of what it takes to get to the desired goal. Planning is vital for success. This includes the next steps when there is opposition and emergencies. In addition to this, a leader needs foresight. Learning from past mistakes will prevent those errors from happening again. History will repeat itself until people learn their lessons. Sometimes you need to trust your gut. When something does not feel right, it is important to speak up, especially if you are an effective follower. Ira Chaleff, an author and speaker wrote a book about being a courageous follower. A follower of this caliber is strong enough to be right, wrong, and different from the leader. Sometimes they will challenge the leader to stand up for what is right. They are willing to risk their position for the betterment of the group. In return, the leader is made aware of his or her faults. This can bring the leader closer because of the accountability. Their intuition lets them know when it is time to take a stand. Maybe the work conditions are horrible. A toxic member might be spreading negative energy all the time while the leader turns a blind eye. Whatever the case may be, the courageous follower is not fearful. The eighth characteristic is stewardship. Taking care of the whole organization. The servant-leader has the responsibility of managing everyone. This is keeping your area clean. Protecting the environment is an example of good stewardship. In school, maybe you had a challenge that involved a prize for the class that recycled the most. Using less plastic and seeking new alternatives have been emphasized more and more over the last few years. Businesses want to be sustainable in the same way. The hunger for success should not last one year, it should be growing for years. People who are good stewards do not hide from change, they welcome it. They get others involved. When you are working in an environment where everyone wants to win, you start to feel the same. Great things happen when everyone is using their skills to the best of their ability. It can change a failing organization into a world-class team. Commitment to the growth of people is essential. This is the ninth characteristic. Picture two little league basketball teams. The players are all eight or nine years old. Team A has a coach that cares more about wins than the development of his players. The regular season consists of ten games. This team goes 5-5. Some of the wins were against teams they knew they were going to beat by a landslide. But each of those five losses could be avoided if the team was more disciplined. If you have ever watched a basketball game at any level, you know there will be some bogus calls. You know going in that the referees will not call every foul. In crunch time, the coach from Team A fails to keep his composure. So what do his players do? They start to show their frustration. Technical fouls left and right, and the star player gets ejected. What happens then? This team is already beat. The players on the bench that did not play as much lack development. In practice they execute but since they lack experience, the team falls apart in the game. Part of committing to the growth of others is allowing them to use their skills to excel. The coach from Team B knows this. He knows that raising the level of skill and chemistry on the team will naturally produce wins. For this reason, they go 9-1. A much better record; a winning record. Why? The coach is committed to his players. This team will stick together. No one will want to leave because of the comradery. In crunch time, this team comes together like it is the beginning of the game. They stick to the plan and trust each other. When they are down, they pick each other up. While the players that give you the best chances of winning should be in the game the most, everyone has a role. There is no star player because anybody can be a star on any given night. The best games are when everyone eats. Last but not least, servant-leaders build community. They bring everyone together and work alongside them. In a grocery store, it would help to have employees from each department meeting to talk about daily and weekly goals. If there is no community, then there is no trust.

Everyone needs to know what their purpose is, as it benefits the store and company as a whole. Why are all these characteristics important? When a leader focuses on the performance and growth of the follower, it leads to success. The performance of the followers directly affects the performance of the organization. What you put in is what you get out. After some time, when everything is done correctly, the organization makes an impact on society. This can motivate new prospects to seek employment. Another result would be attracting players to the team. When people see how you run things, it might spark something in them that makes them want to join. At the least, they can support what you are doing from a distance. When I think about the servant-leaders in my life, I think about the youth pastors I had. Each one of them made it a point to listen to everyone. Some days we would have group discussions where they were preaching and we were listening. On other days we would split into groups by grade where we could share our opinions more. For pastors, having awareness affects the people. If the message is not clicking, maybe they need to shift the focus. When the sermon is receiving high praise, they look to make it better the next week. They want people to be in a different place spiritually when they leave the church after the service. It is the responsibility of the followers to get closer to God. However, they do not walk in their faith alone. The church provides that community that any type of individual needs. Most churches today have life groups that certain people can join. What I mean by certain people is those who are divorced, single parents, newlyweds, fathers, and more. A church with a strong system for toddlers and the youth has foresight. They know if they can plant the seed of the faith early, the child has principles and concepts to rely on later. This is the firm foundation that can change the lives of future generations. Staying on this example, pastors had those leaders that inspired them at a young age. Take a second to think about who inspires you. Who is that person in your life that you would label a servant-leader? Or you can think about someone great at moving people to reach a goal. You see them lead even when you are not there and you see the results. Around this person, you feel safe because of their authenticity. What makes a leader authentic? They are transparent. People trust them because they are true to themselves and others. Authentic leadership is about being ethical. When this style of leadership is present, everyone is advised to share their opinions. Voices are heard and new ideas are discussed. For big decisions that need to be made, the leader provides their opinion, then they open the floor for followers. They do not decide without discussing it with the group first. Any leader can speak about what they do but the difference is the authentic ones lead by example. This is the individual that leads from the front and not the back. When a leader is in the back, they use their voice and their followers go forward. On the other hand, when a leader is in the front, they are moving forward with the group. In battle, they are right there. For major projects in the office, they are right there. In organizations with this type of leader, more people are driven. The level of enthusiasm is heightened because the leader is completely invested. They hold nothing back. I will keep bringing up school as an example because it resonates with me. I have had teachers that brought their hearts to the classroom. I understand that everyone did not have an amazing experience in elementary, middle school, or high school. Some people struggled to graduate, or maybe they dropped out. To illustrate, an authentic leader to me is a kindergarten teacher. If you are a parent, you walk into the classroom and see the result of this style. Pictures and colorful decorations cover the wall. You see the names of every student on their artwork as it hangs on clothespins. Each desk has its name tag. Every so often, the desks are rearranged so students can engage with different people throughout the year. The room has turned into a coloring book that shows how much the teacher cares. There is a carpet with the ABCs and a small library with entertaining books. You can tell that the teacher is committed. Students are engaged and enthusiastic when they walk through the door. This is what you should want if you are a follower. A leader that knows when they are wrong, and admits their mistakes. A person that is okay with criticism and moving accordingly. The one that brings their full self to work consistently is powerful. This is the kindergarten teacher that greets every student, making them feel seen and heard. If you are a parent, this pleases you. You want your kid to be in a safe environment where they can grow. All of this is preferred. Leaders are everywhere. But you are probably still asking yourself. How do I become a leader? Instead of looking for validation externally, look within. You need to be aware of your tendencies, especially the ones that hold you back. Practicing this will put you ahead of most. What you can do today is write down your goals. This is simple. What is that you want to accomplish? I have asked you this before, but take some time to think about what you want. Then think about what you need to do each day to reach them. This is where you create a plan. Another method is meditation. If you are afraid of doing it wrong, then you are mistaken. There is no right way to meditate. You can stare at a wall and think for fifteen minutes. If you want to feel calm, then try some breathing exercises. Asking for feedback from trusted friends can also help you. At a higher level, you can track your habits. Pride gets in the way when trying to become self-aware. If you are successful, you might think you have done nothing wrong. At this point, you believe there is nothing you can do to be better. Be a good listener. Be willing to take criticism and get others involved. A person cannot lead without followers. Make your expectations clear. Without a target, there is nothing to aim at. Be flexible when problems come up because they will. How you handle failure will show your followers how strong or weak you are. Understand that every loss is a learning experience. Never stop learning because it can make or break the organization. Continue to educate yourself because you never know how someone else might process the information you choose to share. Something can click within them that could lead to success. Good communication is often avoided but it is a key player in the performance of others. The unclear needs to be specified. Without a connection to followers, the leader can be egotistic and expectations are not met. When the non-negotiables are introduced in the beginning, it gives followers a roadmap to their work. In an environment with little to no rules, nothing gets done. The productivity is low. This is when you delegate. Each person had a responsibility to keep things flowing. Be the model that your followers need. Lead by your actions. Stay consistent with what you say. Know that there is always something you can improve. This goes for everyone. When you continue to improve, you should not see a limit. Bring your all to the workplace. Motivation others will raise their performance. Some need it more than others. Know what type of followers you have and work to make them all effective in an ethical way. When you need help, ask for it. There is no problem with followers helping leaders. Trusting in their abilities gives them confidence. The most memorable leaders in my life never avoided communication. They made it a point to highlight their mistakes. With every loss, they adjusted. They have a people-first mindset. What benefits others is at the top of their priority list. Building community is what keeps members on the team. When you do not want to win with anyone else, great things happen. Player and employee retention will decide whether or not the foundation stays solid. Healthy relationships are built under a leader that serves while being authentic. As a result, followers who do choose to leave can teach the same principles to their future followers. Leadership is learned. No one is born with it. But anyone who works at it will be successful. Do not accept your limiting beliefs. You can become a leader in your community. If you are not one yet, you can take the steps to get there. Your choices will either keep you stuck or help you level up. Be aware of your actions. Adjust to the resistance. Become the leader you needed when you were younger.

CHAPTER 14

REINVENT YOURSELF

How well do you know yourself? You are the only one that knows exactly what you eat, how you sleep and go through the day. When you look in the mirror, you can feel shame or gratitude. Maybe both at the same time. What goes through your mind when you wake up? Unless you are living your dream life, you feel unfulfilled. You see people around you living successfully and something inside you is envious. What are your values? What are the bad habits that seem to hold you back? Only you can answer those questions. Through years of conditioning, maybe your limiting beliefs have compounded. How you were raised and where you were raised had an impact on you. Whether you had both parents, one parent, or an older relative taking care of you, this is how your identity was formed. The activities you enjoyed in school to the friends you still keep around today. All of it, from birth to this day has made you who you are. After the rise of social media, you had access to millions of people. The ones who are efficient in their professions have been highlighted. This is external. What you think about yourself can be the difference between toxic and meaningful relationships. You can tell who respects themselves by the way they operate. Their posture when they walk is one sign. If they have their shoulders rounded while staring at the ground, it could be that they have low self-esteem. When you go to talk to someone like this, they might not hold good eye contact. Maybe they are unsure of the words that come out of their mouths. Having good posture is one small part of life that can keep you healthy. This keeps your spine aligned and muscle fatigue is eliminated. Lower back pain is reduced, which is something that can harm anybody. The person who walks tall and confident feels better. Their head is up and their shoulders are back. When a man walks into an area as if he owns it, people around cannot help themselves. Bystanders start to think, "Who does this guy think he is?" as he takes step after step. The same goes for women. Confidence is attractive. When you see someone that walks this way, you start to trust them. They have a sense of direction. There is something positive going on internally with this person. Even if they are going through tough times, you can hardly tell. So think about what you want to change. What is something you do not like about yourself? Be honest. Write it down, all unfiltered. Let it all out on the paper. What can you change? After you completed this list, separate what you can control from what you cannot. Here is a refresher of things you can control: your attitude, effort, work ethic, network, physique, thoughts, and diet. While the list can be longer, these are the just basic parts of life that can make you successful. Attitude. Something that can turn a rainy day into a sunny one. This changes the way you attack responsibilities. Instead of saying "I have to go to work" you say "I get to go to work." This is a common idea that is shared by a fair amount of motivational speakers and leaders. People will know how great your attitude is when you face minor or major inconveniences. This is where you must be grateful. I am not trying to gaslight your situation. We all go through hardships and there should be no comparison. With that being said, it could be worse. Attitude can alter your performance. If you have played sports, in a band, or even remembered a fun class from school. There was always that classmate or teammate with a bad attitude. They could be so much more than they are if they had the right attitude. You see them waste their potential and get nothing done by complaining. Attitude changes the way you see. What looks like an unsolvable problem to most can look like an opportunity for growth to you. This leads to the effort. When it comes to your job and other aspects that require commitment, your effort matters. There are three areas on the spectrum where people camp. One area is all in. This person brings their A-game at all times. You would think that this person never rests like they have no off switch. On a scale from one to ten, they are on eleven daily. Their energy is contagious. This is the person that is willing to go to war with everybody. You might know someone like this. If you are like this, more power to you. Keep going. When you raise your effort levels, people notice. They might not applaud you. This is when you must applaud yourself. Not everyone is there in the dark with you to appreciate the time you put in. The other side of this is the person that is all out. Picture a group of four people holding hands and getting ready to jump into a pool. Three of them are like the person I described. They are all in and ready to jump. But the one person is comfortable where they are. So when it is time to go, they hold back at the last second. This person is all out. As soon as this happens, they make excuses as to why they decided not to commit. They might have dipped their toes in the pool or walked down the steps. One foot in the pool does not fully submerge your body. In everything you do, your amount of effort predicts the results you get. I know you have heard the common phrase, "you get out what you put in." So why not? There is something internally or externally that is blocking you from reaching your version of the top. We will continue this example. Say the person walks down the steps into the pool. Now they are in the water up to their waist. For the time being, they are in the three-foot area. In the third area lies those who are lukewarm. Around Christmas, kids enjoy candy canes and hot chocolate. It is called hot chocolate for a reason, not lukewarm chocolate. When a person is lukewarm, they show no enthusiasm. They lack conviction. At their convenience, they decide when to be enthusiastic. This is the person that only shows up when they feel like it. You cannot count on them because you never know when they will show up. On great days, they are firing on all cylinders and put their all into work. On the bad days, they are a no-show. This is the middle of the spectrum. You do not want to be lukewarm. If you are lukewarm in one area, it will soon spill over to other areas in your life. Relationships, your health, and many more. Work ethic. You can teach it by leading by example, but it is something that everyone needs to work on. You need to experience it for yourself. An individual with a strong work ethic focuses on every task and completes each one with the best effort. Even in their failure, they do not stop. Deadlines are met. This person shows up early and can be the last one to leave. In life, punctuality is important. Being on time can take you far. This shows that you value not only your time but the place you work for. Showing that you care makes those around you respect you. When you are the parent, or couple that shows up for the activities that your child participates in, they love you. The engagement is there. Your work ethic could get you in the right circles. More people who share the same values will be included in your circle. This is when you upgrade your network. You have probably heard this phrase from authors, speakers, or people you know. Your network is your net worth. Who you hang around can help or harm you. Motivational speaker Jim Rohn stated, "you're the average of the five people you spend the most time with." If you do not believe this then look at your circle. What happens when you hang around them? Most people do not consider this because they have known them for so long. The people in lazy circles do not want to see anyone win. Once you start leveling up, there is a high chance that they will start to envy you. Take your physique for example. If all of your friends are overweight, lack self-respect, and overeat all the time, then you will do the same. Birds of a feather flock together. You need to know when to leave the flock. What you eat, how often you exercise, and the sleep you get affects your physique. These are three things you can change. If you have forgotten about the contents of your diet, go back and reread that chapter. Lastly, your thoughts. They predict your future. Thoughts lead to actions. Frequent actions are your habits. If they are unhealthy, you will be unhealthy. When you feed your mind positivity, you will show gratitude for the things you take for granted. This is why you should practice writing down everything you are grateful for. I repeat this because it changes the way you see life. This is called gratitude journaling. You decide how much you practice this. It could be every day or once a week. Start your morning doing this. It is better to begin the day grateful rather than dragging through. You do not deserve to live in constant stress. Practicing as much as you can provide you the skill of seeing the silver lining in every dark cloud. These are some of the things you can control. This chapter is about reinventing yourself. So how do you do it? What does it mean to reinvent yourself? Understanding yourself is the first step. For starters, it is defining what you are great at and what you need to work on. Even if it is embarrassing, you need to work on your weaknesses. We like to work on our strengths because it makes us look good. People see us working on our strengths and believe it is effortless. But this skill that you have took time. Similarly, it will take some time to reinvent yourself. Part of this process is evaluating and replacing. You need to evaluate all of your habits and values. See how they have changed your life. Say you want to lose weight. A common goal for millions of people. What you need to do is look at your diet. Look at the food you buy and what you snack on throughout the day. Maybe you have some belly fat that you want to shed before a certain time. What you eat and the amount of calories you eat affects your weight. Then you partner this with a regular exercise schedule. You can start small, the important thing is that you take the first step. If you have a busy schedule, work out in the morning. For those that have no time throughout the day, work out at night. A thirty-minute walk on the treadmill is a good start. This is what makes the gym an exciting place. People from different backgrounds use the same space to reach different goals. All walks of life. Old and young. This is the replacing phase. You go an exercise instead of streaming your favorite movies and tv shows. The extra time you have can be used to plan meals. It is easy to eat fast-food all the time. A person who wants to reinvent themselves in this area must be disciplined. One thing that you can always control is your discipline. When the motivation is not there, you need to rely on your mission. If your goal was to lose weight, then there is no excuse when you do not feel like working out. The more excuses you give yourself, the less progress you will make. If you allow your excuses to hold you back, you will always find a reason why you cannot succeed. Exercising is something you do not rush into. Taking gradual steps toward more challenging routines is what you should do. Who do you want to be? Where do you want to be? This is when you need to define your values. Whatever you have faith in, stand firm in it. Make the nonnegotiable known. Without values, you can lose your sense of direction. You might make exceptions just because it feels good at the moment. But that is harming your growth. The people you associate with, the places you go; it all matters. You feel some sense of emptiness inside from a few of the activities you are engaging in. So you continue to try to fill that void through unhealthy practices. Yet you can still turn this around. You can change your lifestyle for the better. Do it for yourself. Think of ways you can make progress each day. If you do this consistently, you will thank yourself later for sticking to the plan. Especially through hardships because they will come. Another activity you can try is learning a new skill. Sometimes we need to be humbled. We need to understand that it is okay to be a beginner and learn from others. After acquiring new skills, you might fall in love with them. You could find your purpose this way. Experimenting in different areas like writing music, creating art, selling products, and more. Reinvention does not happen when you are alone. While you can go through this journey alone, you will not go far without others. This needs to be ingrained in your mind. Get help from people more successful than you. It expands your network which can lead to a higher net worth. If you are currently in a rut. Ask yourself why that is. The sum of all the people in your environment might be a key factor. What you do when no one is watching is an even bigger contributor to your feelings. Instead of wishing for that dream, work for it. This requires you to leave your comfort zone that is so heavily promoted today. The world wants you to live in comfort. But you were not meant to be living this way. No matter who you are, you were meant to face challenges head-on. In comfort, you cannot do that. The first journal entry I ever wrote was titled *The Look and Feel of Success*. I wrote this on July 1, 2021. After I bought the journal I searched the internet for journaling exercises. I found this video from a creator with thousands of subscribers. The look and feel of success is a writing prompt that allows you to describe that dream. Knowing what you want success to look like is important. Predicting how you will feel also helps. Even though what you accomplish might not feel like you wanted, it is a great reference. The next step in this prompt was to identify the barriers. What is something or someone that is in the way of you reaching those goals? You write down one or two barriers for each goal. Then you write down ways to overcome those barriers. This is essentially your plan of action. You refer back to this when you feel like you are going in the wrong direction. A feeling of joy should come over you as you write this. After all, this is your goal and your version of the dream life. Having an idea of where you want to go will help you come up with more ideas. There is more than one way to get there. Now that you know that, you take different steps. You cannot aim at a target if the target is not there. Dragging through the days is not going to get you there. Wasting time and money on harmful activities will not get you there if you become addicted. This is where the internal game comes into play. Being honest with yourself is mandatory. No sugar-coating. This can be hard for some because of the lack of accountability. But you must take ownership of where you are right now. All the decisions you made have compounded. You can hide this from others, but you cannot hide this from yourself. When you take responsibility you get the power to change. Your thought patterns are different. They shift from a feeling of being stuck in a situation to creating solutions to get out. The victim mentality that might have been established in early childhood starts to leave. An individual with a victim mentality blames everyone. They choose not to take responsibility. As far as the control in their life goes, they feel like they have none. The truth is you do not have control over what people say or do to you. You cannot control their thoughts either. Whether you succeed or not, people will always have something to say. They could try to limit you or downplay your success. Do not get lost in this. What are they doing? If they were not miserable in their lives, then they would not be projecting their insecurities on you. People who are working to reach their goals might show more support. Since they understand the time it takes, they will resonate with your story and what you are doing. When you are putting in the work daily, you are already ahead of most. If you are serious about your dreams, you know they are above average. The life you envision should be well above average. If you have thought about this then you are not like most people. So why should you settle? What worked for me was making goals for each month. Then I went further by writing down goals for the year. This applies pressure. Remember, starting is great. Staying consistent can be challenging. But once you cross that finish line once, you hunger for more. Once you reach one goal, you set more. Make it a pattern and you will be living that dream life sooner than you think. Going back to the previous journaling exercise, more barriers will pop up. The ones you list might go away, while new ones show themselves. A key sign that you are doing well in life is you have greater discernment. Whatever the situation is, you know what serves you and what does not. You can easily recognize what is in front of you and see if you want it. This will widen the gap between you and the average company you keep. What you used to do does not excite you anymore because you overindulged. This is okay. Another sign is knowing your passions. You have a strong desire for the activities that make you happy. No matter what, you try to set aside some time to work on this passion.

Being appreciative of this activity changes your attitude. If you have nothing else to wake up for, this is it. Your passion gives you additional direction. For the beginning stages of self-improvement, you are going to have to put the blinders on. As far as you are concerned, what other people are doing is not important. Unless their actions align with your goals, you should not focus on them. This is where many people mess up. They focus on what works for others and not themselves. Do not forget that this is your journey. What worked for someone else might not work for you. I will bring up meditation again. There are millions of results you can get when you search for meditation tips. Certain religions might show up when you search online. Just because a one-hour session worked for one person does not mean you should jump in and do the same. Gradual progress is still progress. Set a timer for thirty seconds or a minute. See if you can focus on little things like your breath. Try a guided meditation and see where that takes you mentally. Adjust the time. What worked for me when I first started was closing my eyes and focusing on my breath for fifteen minutes. I did this weekly for a couple of months. Then I adjusted the timer to twenty minutes for a few weeks. Eventually, I timed my longest meditation session at forty-one minutes and twenty-three seconds. I share this to let you know that I was a beginner at this. At first, I thought it would not affect me. But my mental health was on a steady level when I kept practicing. When I meditated, each day was different. I had a new thing or person to be grateful for in my life. I appreciated the work I was doing. While being highly self-aware, I was not hard on myself. The negative self-talk was replaced with positive affirmations. You are worthy of overwhelming success. When you believe in yourself, you have a chance. When you work at what you want, you have an even better chance. Reinventing yourself is a lifestyle change. Switching from your old ways to new ways is an internal battle. You will go to war against yourself most days. Embrace it. Fall in love with the process. How do you achieve this? What if you are attached to the result more than the process? What you can do today is stay in the present. The results will not be there the next day. But it could be the next month or year. You decide based on consistency. Find value in your efforts. Just because you have not accomplished that goal does not mean you should not reward yourself. In times when you work with no audience cheering you on, you need to clap for yourself. Be your biggest fan. The fact that you are making progress is amazing. This is something you can celebrate. It is in the process that you learn to enjoy the steps. The harder days teach you lessons while giving you hope. When you have hope for the future, you are not as anxious. You look forward to the next day because every day is an opportunity for growth. The focus shifts to the process. Your days start to line up with what you want in the next five years, ten years, and twenty years. If you want to take this to an extreme level, set a date. Highlight the date on your calendar when you will accomplish one goal. This will create a sense of urgency. Even if you do not reach it, you will be much closer because you gave yourself less time. For those that work well under pressure, this can help. If you want to take smaller steps, go ahead. But you cannot put off the work. In my experience, the process is fun. To this day, there are times when I find it hard not to focus on the result. I forget to appreciate how much progress I have made. The finish line in my head continues to move. However, this will not completely limit your success. When you cross one goal off your list, it is okay to set bigger ones. Do not be satisfied. Being complacent will keep you comfortable. If you want to reach the high levels that you talk about, you cannot stay in your comfort zone. Too many people fail to take ownership and action in their life. They lack commitment. Surely you will not follow the crowd. There are plenty of people with the same growth mindset as you. Connect with them. Build relationships. Prioritize your life. Find a way. Choose the process that works best for you. Reinvent yourself. Appreciate where you are today, then execute. Run your race.

CHAPTER 15

ENJOY THE MOMENT

Why is it so hard to stay present? You are here now, reading this book. But where is your mind at? You are on a mission. Some days are busier than others. Every day you have a choice. You can choose to start your day distracted or focused. Instant gratification is addicting. More ways to be comfortable and seek entertainment are being shared daily. The world is at our fingertips. We stream and scroll without taking a breath. After one activity, we immediately move to the next. We want to be in the know. Our idea of being at the top includes social media. Make the best posts at the best times to get the most likes. Collect the most possessions to gain more friends. We want to look like we have it all together. The slightest bit of weakness we show gets shared across friend groups. We are afraid of being abandoned and disliked. So we do what we can to get as much attention and validation from everyone. We want to stay connected to our friends and family. Some of us have a fear of missing out. Also known as FOMO. The latest everything; we want it all. The average person wakes up, checks their phone, and starts scrolling. People who do this are setting themselves up for failure. All the information and stimulation being flooded through the mind can cause stress. Watching the news, while informative also has the same effect. Being overwhelmed with loads of information before you start your day can blur your focus.

Maybe your emotions are dependent on the number of friends you have, the likes you get, and the money you earn. So you are stuck in a race with no finish line. You are chasing one level of gratification after the next. This hurts you. Deep down you want to be happy but you are unfulfilled. The company you keep might be negative. Maybe you need to take a break from social media so you can stop comparing yourself to others. Staying present improves your mental health. Past events still have a hold on you when you are depressed. Staring too far into the future is where your anxiety comes from. How do you enjoy the moment? You do this by being present. One step you can take is removing distractions. The biggest distractions today come from our phones. We have access to so much, and sometimes we need to limit our time spent. You cannot get wasted time back. Put your phone in another room before you go to bed. Try using an actual alarm. Turn off the tv at least two hours before sleeping. In this time that you usually spend watching, you can sit in silence. When you are alone, mind your thoughts. It is easy to let your mind wander. This can cause you to make up scenarios that might not ever happen. Old memories might trigger you and send you to a dark place. You could be stressing over places you have not explored or people you have not talked to yet. Let go of the past by accepting what happened. Remind yourself that you cannot go back and fix things. In life, you may have ugly starts, but it is how you finish. If you have learned nothing from the past, then you are bound to repeat the same mistakes. When your identity is in the past, you will not grow. You will continue to act like that younger version of yourself. A good way to combat this is to spend time with those who make you happy. I am referring to those that fit your future. You do this by reaching out. We like to stay in our bubbles. Maybe we hang out with those doing far worse than us so we can feel better about ourselves. This will limit you. I am sure you have heard the quote, "If you are the smartest in the room, you are in the wrong room!" This still rings true today. Too many people are hanging around individuals that do not think big, dream big, or take action. All they do is talk about what they want to do. They have no plan. Taking control of their life scares them, so they live comfortably and complain. You should not be in the same area as them. Executing your plans and doing what you say you are going to do will automatically separate you from the majority. Avoid worrying about things out of your control. When you worry less, you have more time to appreciate the little things. Even if you are not happy about where you are now, you can acknowledge the progress you are making. When I first started getting serious about fitness, I was not happy about my physique. I would watch videos and read articles from credible websites that included workout ideas. In middle school, I started doing body weight exercises. No equipment, just me. Some nights I would do twenty-five push-ups before bed. Then I did fifty, then one hundred. I wanted to get rid of my bird chest so I did as many push-ups as I could. Eventually, I was able to bench press my weight and extra. For sit-ups and squats, I followed the same formula. When I was able to perform every compound lift, I entered a season of progressive overload. In weight training, progressive overload means you increase the number of repetitions performed or increase the weight slowly. With every set, you are increasing the intensity. It gets harder and your body must adjust. This is trying a weight that you can only lift six to eight times and going for ten to twelve reps. Soon, you will be able to see the gains. In the same way, you need to use the progressive overload approach to your dreams. Develop the mindset of pushing a little harder each day. Even if it is one more rep, you have the strength to go through it. While being under loads of stress is not great for your long-term health, you need some of that to build you. For weight training, after the workout, your muscle fibers break down. The recovery period involves those muscle fibers rebuilding and becoming stronger. By the next workout, that weight gets easier and easier. This is what happens when you put in the work in your specialized area. If you want to get there in all areas, then this method will need to be applied to everything you do. What do you do from the time you wake up to the time you lay your head down on the pillow? All of these actions add up. While it is great to monitor your steps, sometimes you will fall short. Taking yourself too seriously can drive you to control the uncontrollable. I know from experience that it hurts more when you try to take care of everything. Your time is valuable, but that does not mean you should isolate yourself for long periods. This is not to say that disconnecting from negative people and social media is bad. There is a difference. To take your mind off yourself, you can perform random acts of kindness. For example, paying for the food ordered by the person behind you at the drive-thru. This can be tipping your waitress more than usual. Maybe you can make it a goal to compliment one stranger daily. You are not holding in the positivity, you are spreading it. The world can always use more positivity. We get wrapped in our worlds and refuse to interact with others. It is okay to put yourself out there. Not everyone will agree with you or your methods. Sometimes they might reject you and ask you why you seem to be so happy. Do not let the negative voices ruin your mission. There is a light inside you and it needs to be shared with others. You have a gift and many talents that can help you reach your full potential. Combine this with your passion and you will succeed. One thing that many people suffer from is destination addiction. This is when a person believes that happiness and success are destinations. They choose to delay their happiness. They use phrases like, "I'll be happy when this happens" or "Happiness can be found in the future but not in the present." Unfortunately, they are never content with life. When they finally reach a goal, they feel empty. One accomplishment after the next, they are left unsatisfied. Many people wait until they get into relationships, careers, or earn a certain amount of money to be happy. The pain is found in their expectations. It is good to have expectations but know that they will not always be met. Plans can fall through and you will have to make decisions on the fly. This is a part of life that you cannot avoid. I had a problem with destination addiction when I got into lifting. When I saw the progress that others were making, I wanted the same. My records were fair, but I was not satisfied. I set higher goals and every time, I delayed my happiness until I reached them. This was not good for me mentally. I spent no time enjoying my progress. When I would receive compliments, I thought to myself, "I can do better." After lifting more than twice my weight, I still felt weak. I focused on the wrong things. I thought from the beginning that the respect I would receive was contingent on the amount of weight I lifted. Sometimes I would lift every day of the week. This was my way of escaping. On the other side of this is staying content. An individual who accomplishes a goal and is satisfied either forever or for a long period is wasting their potential. Boasting about accomplishments from the past takes away from the execution of today. Chances are if you are bragging about it, you do not intend to go any further. This is the climber that reaches the top of the mountain, looks at the other mountains in the distance, and says "I am okay right here." This is a marathon. But they chose to stay at their level and not try to get better.

Their ego tells them that they have already improved and are at their best. To improve means leaving their comfort zone and they will do whatever it takes not to. Try not to become this person. Be obsessed with the process, not the results. When you do not get the results you want, change the plan, not the goal. You took a different approach when maybe all you need is a slight change. One step forward after the other, until you win. While exercise is great for your mental and overall health, you still need community. This applies to whatever your passion is. You need to be in contact with positive people. On your self-improvement journey, going after new experiences will teach you a few things. Visiting a new city or country can broaden your horizon. Sometimes we get so used to our style of living and think that everyone lives that way. When we meet these people we might start judging. In conversation, we fail to understand the person speaking. We all come from different families and backgrounds. Different experiences have made us who we are and how we think. Shared experiences build self-esteem. When families go on vacation, you see that they are happy to get away. If they have small children, they take more pictures than usual. They are savoring the moment. They at least look like they are enjoying their time together. Despite the disasters around the world, these experiences decrease your anxiety. When you are too focused on the present, you do not have time to worry about the past. You simply enjoy the activities and keep finding ways to feel good. Be in the zone, at work, at home, and everywhere you go. In the 1970s Hungarian-American psychologist Mihaly Csikszentmihalyi came up with the concept of flow. Also known as flow theory. We know this today as the flow state. When an individual is in a flow state, they are fully immersed in what they are doing. This is the bridge between skills and challenge. When experiencing this, you complete tasks with no effort. You lose track of time in a flow state. The most important part about this is that you are all the way present. You are locked in on one goal. Being in this mental state does not mean you do the work without feeling good. Mentally, it is enjoyable. The activity brings you joy with some natural resistance. Without resistance, you cannot grow. So when you have fun doing the activity, you feel more connected to the process. How do you get into a flow state? You need to start by getting rid of all distractions. Keep your phone away from you, turn the ringer off, and get to work. Next, you need to have clear goals.

What do you want to get out of this session? What needs to be done while you work? A key strategy is not thinking about it, just doing it. To fully immerse yourself, you need to be focused for around fifteen minutes or more. Similar to meditation, you will get off track sometimes. The first time will not be perfect. Line up your responsibilities in order of importance. Do the task that will take the most time first, then move from there. There are plenty of benefits that you will receive. One of them is intrinsic motivation. This is doing something that makes you feel good. An example would be your passion. Something that you would do for free. When you are doing what you love, it also brings out your creativity. Creativity is the next benefit. When you enter a flow state, ideas might start flying. Learning how to harness these ideas and act on them can be the tougher part. Multitasking will not help you in this area. Create a block schedule if you need to. For ninety minutes, focus on the first task, take a short break, then go to the next. Understand that you are efficient now, but you can be better in the future. The opposite of this is extrinsic motivation. A simple example is being paid to do a job for someone or a company. An individual with extrinsic motivation is there to do their job because it pays the bills. While not glamorous or joyful, they get the work done for forty or more hours weekly. Another benefit is the learning aspect. When you go through this a few times, you learn what works. The conditions for the most part are under your control. You can change your environment to best suit you. This is going to take some trial and error. You are not being thrown into the fire, as you are not forcing yourself. But to get in the right mindset for this at least means you are up for the challenge. Proving others wrong can be exhilarating, but proving yourself right is priceless. By frequently being in a flow state, you can prevent feelings of burnout that can lead to depression. You will feel tired but not exhausted. Splitting up your work in blocks or days can take the load off. One day might be the best amount of time to accomplish everything, but it can lower productivity for others. If you could build an empire in one day, then that empire is not great. Sure you can rush the process and focus on everything at the same time. But where does that leave you? It will expose your weakness in some areas. When you rush the process, your deficiencies will show. Day by day you need to put your energy toward one area. Then use the following days to rotate between areas. A week of consistency can set you up for success in a month. A few months of dedicated work will set you up for a successful year. It takes some getting used to. Bringing all your energy and focus into one thing is hard. But this is a must if you want to go beyond your limit. If you are starving for a win, you must adopt this technique. The flow state is a short period where you enjoy the moment. You will want to conquer more. Getting motivation from outside sources does not last long. When it is intrinsic, when you enjoy it, you cannot help but give it all you got. Anything less can be defined as average, mediocre even. You will not waste your time being distracted. Instead, you will use your downtime by either relaxing or thinking of ways to make the next experience better. Flow states do not happen if the individual is not enjoying what they are doing. Taking orders in a drive-thru, stocking groceries, or cleaning up popcorn might not be the dream for some people. This is what they have to do so they can one day spend more time on their dreams. They are extrinsically motivated. Maybe this is you. You might work nine to five every day and believe you have no time. But you do. The early mornings and evenings can be used to get one step closer. Going back to the community. In an efficient business, everyone has their roles and they perform well. When you walk in, you can tell that everything is on point. The attention to detail is there and you see that everyone is getting their job done. So if you cannot enter a flow state alone; try with a company. When the distractions are eliminated, there is room to talk. You might be in a flow state without knowing it. This can get you through group projects and study sessions. Everyone is on the same page but has different goals. Knowing that others can be struggling might motivate you to get them there. At the same time, they are there to assist you. Sometimes you will not have all the answers. In a group setting, you can call upon each other with pure intentions. Everyone wants to be great, but few take the next step. You could be holding yourself back when you reject outside input. In some cases, you will need that extra boost to push you. But you have to want it. The flow state gives you mental clarity. Who does not want mental clarity? In this life of uncertainty, it would be amazing to have a few moments of clarity. Right? This builds your confidence. Something everyone can use some more of. You are alert. You are in control even though it feels like you are in auto pilot mode. Quality work comes from the flow. There is not an overwhelming amount of anxiety due to deadlines. You are in control. The flow state is just one theory proven to be effective in the workplace and daily life. Maybe you need some practical strategies that you can try today. Everyone likes quick step-by-step guides. We like results to be instant so we do the things that give us instant results. From experience, this takes some practice. But it will not take you forever. The following activities can bring joy to anyone that works at them. You might find something that you like. The first activity I recommend is exercise. No matter the level of intensity, you can improve your overall health. Mentally, your brain releases endorphins that make you feel good. At the least, you can do yoga and deep breathing exercises. Physically, you can shed some pounds and build strength. If you do not have a gym membership, then you can take a walk in nature. Being out of the house and breathing fresh air is what you need sometimes. If you enjoy this then you can also try gardening. Being connected to your surroundings can reduce stress. When you have something to care for, like a plant, you want to do it correctly. You water it, give it proper sunlight, and hope for the best. Just like your dreams, you have planted the seed. When you put in the time, you get to enjoy the fruits of your labor. If you want to expand your palette, try cooking. Specifically cooking a new dish that you have never tried before. The smells and tastes of your work can be appreciated by others. You might not get it right on the first try. Remember that you can become great at whatever you put your mind to. Even if it is a simple dish. Sitting down and having a meal that you created is far better than fast-food. Imagine how much fun you could have if you ditch the classic meals and make one of your own. After the meal is prepared, you get to enjoy your hard work. Then when you are skilled at making that one dish or dessert, you will try other recipes. Maybe you will amen your recipe. Cooking allows you to be mindful of the number of ingredients used. Too much of one ingredient might overpower the whole dish. But too little of that ingredient might not make it complete. If it tastes bland, then it needs some more seasoning. This is a quick solution if you want your food to taste great. Go easy on yourself if it is your first time. Being mindful is something that most people fail to practice. We are creatures of habit and we like what feels good. Staying in our boxes plays a role in our overall health. Without meaningful relationships, we can feed into the lies our minds tell us. You might think you are not worthy of connection. But you are. Everyone deserves to be in contact with people that fulfill them. Truthfully, you can be present in everything you do. Whether you are washing the dishes or running a marathon, you can be there. One quote that I have heard from multiple influencers in my life is "Be where your feet are." In times of doubt and unrest, I think about this quote. I believe you should too. We are all guilty of being there, but not there. Sometimes we miss out on memories because we are in a different place mentally. We might pretend that we are in good spirits but deep down, we are discouraged. To be where your feet are means you bring your all. The people around you that you care about should see love to see you happy. When you are involved in their lives, pouring into them, they will pour into you. If they are not, then you need to rethink the value of those relationships. But if they are, cherish them. Most friends will be there to give you support and try to motivate you. Real friends know when to pick you up when you fall. Authentic friends are not afraid to call you out when something is off. Through shared experiences, you do not have to take your journey alone. There is strength in numbers. You need to be aware of the signs that you are not present in your life. The first and most relatable is your mind. Throughout the day, your mind is going a thousand miles an hour. Your thoughts keep you up at night. Were you good enough today? Did you finish everything on your list? Does your partner love you? What will people think? Are you eating right? How is your family? How are you coping? All of these questions might be flooding your mind when you try to rest. Wondering if you did your best. Questioning your ability to get the job done. It happens to all of us. You need quality sleep. One night of poor sleep can ruin your days and weeks. If it becomes a habit, then you can live fatigued. Another sign is your lack of enthusiasm for activities you used to enjoy. Nothing you do seems fun. Because you are living in the past or looking too far in the future, the present does not excite you. The fact that you are not where you want to be in life also affects you. We are constantly chasing our version of greatness. Sometimes we forget how much progress we made because we compare ourselves to others. We let the outside noise take control of our lives. The inner voice needs to be recognized. Internal dialogue is also known as the voice in your head. This is how you communicate with yourself throughout the day. Everyone has this. Some voices are louder than others. Positive self-talk will put you ahead. At the very least, you will have a chance against the roadblocks in life. Here is a routine you should try. Every morning when you use the bathroom, look yourself in the mirror and say, "I am confident. I am strong." This is all you need to say to yourself. Think of this as your temporary motto. Add this to your routine. This could change your perspective. Nobody wants to live a miserable life. When you are around people that are wasting their potential, you see how they work. They are trained individuals. Even though you are not responsible for the happiness of others, you can be that light. We all need positive people around us. Maybe not at all times, but most times. You are driven. Maybe that part of you is not awake yet. But the time is now. At the end of each day or week, it is calming to know that you gave your all. The fact that you did not hold back is impressive. Most people conserve their energy by giving into their limiting beliefs. The average person quits as soon as things get hard. But not you. Right? You are confident. You are strong. Believe it. Before you go to sleep, say that same phrase. Change the wors if you need to. Instead of listening to the world, listen to yourself. The world will not always give you the answers you need. True change starts within. When you make a conscious decision to push harder, you move further. Remember when you were just a kid, playing outside in the front yard. Maybe you were running in circles or chasing your older siblings. Throwing the ball around, playing fetch with your dog. Riding bikes with your friends around the neighborhood. At school, hang on the monkey bars and laugh with your classmates. Playing tag with everyone on the playground. Seeing who could run the fastest. During recess or the summer, I imagine you were not thinking about your life right now. You were not discussing financial plans and credit scores at age five. Why? Because you were present. You made memories with your friends. Some of them who you are still close to today. Throughout your years of education, you made lifelong friends. Lasting connections with others created a part of who you are today. Now you look back and miss the "good days." The days when you were not worried about your job, finances, and relationships. You cannot go back. The memories and connections are still there. We are not meant to stay in the same place. We are here to grow. You will drive yourself crazy when you are always looking back. I am not telling you to put the blinders on. But some of the things you want out of this life require intense focus. Do the activities that make you laugh. Enjoy life from this new perspective. Of course, you are not where want to be. Do not be discouraged. In the process, you will find yourself exhausted to the point of quitting. Mindfulness is overlooked because we fill our time by living in the past and future. We find excuses as to why we are not exceeding our standards. You receive a feeling of purpose and drive. Being present allows you to account for your emotions. Your ears are more open to others. This helps you notice your surroundings. You start to appreciate everything and everyone more. As they are not here for no reason either. Managing your stress in this day and age is vital. You cannot skip this. Decide to stay present in not only your life but others as well. Be where your feet are. You are strong. You are confident. Give it your all.

CHAPTER 16

DON'T FORGET TO DREAM

B
e unrealistic. Some people in your life that are usually older will tell
you to be realistic. Parents might want you to take a secure job that
will pay you the average salary. They tell you this because they
believe it worked for them. The resources you have today were not heavily
used when you were growing up. Society has evolved since then. Teachers
might have given you an assignment that involved you sharing your dream
with the class. The classic question "What do you want to be when you
grow up?" You answered. Maybe you wanted to be a singer, actor, actress,
professional basketball player, doctor, veterinarian, or teacher. Sadly, some
teachers bring in the stats when it comes to your dreams. Only one percent
do this, or only ten percent do that. Rightfully so. But this can kill your
confidence. If there is anything that people who strive for greatness need
more of, it is confidence. You can see how people glow when they are sure
of themselves. When they believe in themselves, they make it known.
Children who ride a bike or swim on their own for the first time are
excited. They bring the energy and it shows when they smile. Coaches, for
example, the ones who only care about wins and not developing their
players are contributors. A kid might lose their love for the game. On the
other hand, they can use that horrible experience to find a new team and
excel there. Your friend group is subject to this type of energy too. When

you share your goals you might be greeted with negativity. I say greeted because it can come in the form of backhanded compliments and disbelief. Your friends might ask "You want to do that?" They question your ability. It is possible that they are threatened by your potential and their envy starts to creep in. Random people and coworkers might do the same. They are rooting for you until you succeed. Then they treat you like an enemy when you level up. Now, there is a responsibility to be reasonable when it comes to goal-setting. Reasonable just means sound judgment; being logical. Being realistic means you are basing your goals on what is real or practical. Why are people telling us to be realistic? They could be projecting their insecurities. Around you, they feel weak. They lack ambition. Maybe they have tried and failed and then never tried again. Your vision is for you to keep. Not everyone will understand you and that is okay. It is not their job to. You need to dream big. Too many people go through life wondering "what if" and you should not do the same. Dreams die when people stop working toward them. They lose their hunger, they become satisfied with average living. So they put themselves in a box, hang around with the same people, and never add value to their environment. This should not be the description of the life you want. First, you need to know how to dream big. This is fairly simple. You cannot achieve great things without believing in yourself. No belief, no risk-taking, and no reward. You need to be confident when no one else is. Next, you need to visualize your success. I have repeatedly told you to visualize the life you want because it is important for your growth. This is your target. After doing this, you need to let go of the fear. Simple to say, harder to act out. Average people go through life without facing their fears. There are some common fears that you might have. Fear of failure, death, disease, heights, or tight spaces. These are relevant because you need to know that you are not the only one with fears. People deal with them differently but that does not make you an outlier. Public speaking might be a weakness for you. Picture a kid on the high dive at a waterpark. This kid has a fear of heights but he decided to muster up the courage to walk up to each step. He looks down at the water for a couple of seconds then quickly walks back. As he turns around, he sees the long line behind him. He is already up there, so he should jump. Some jump in and come back out. He finally decides to jump in and he is happy that he did. The longer you wait, the harder it will be to start. You will not be prepared for every little thing that happens. Put yourself in the best position to win by facing your fears. If you wait until you are ready, nothing will get done. You will never be "ready", it is a matter of taking action or not. However, preparation is key. Good preparation will take some of the weight off. Jump when it is uncomfortable. Just like a kid jumping off a high dive, you will adjust to new conditions. The conditions, in this case, are the cold water and time in the air. The time is now. No one likes to adjust on the fly. But if you master this skill, you will accomplish great things. Then, you need to make your limiting belief clear. What do you believe about yourself that holds you back? How do you cope with failure? Dreaming big leaves a positive impact on society. New technology is created. Bluetooth appliances to all-electric vehicles. Someone had a dream to make life easier for companies, employees, and citizens. The phone in your hand and the various devices in your household were once dreams. The connection we have to others in our community was once an idea. Non-profits that benefit those in need. Projects that build up cities. Groundbreaking discoveries in the world of science. People spend their time venturing out to achieve their goals. This gives you a new perspective. When you dream big, new ideas are revealed. Collaboration with others will increase the ideas exponentially. With this, there is higher connectivity. Not only between cities but between countries. In the business world, some want to become the next CEO of a Fortune 500 company. Maybe you want to own a professional team someday. Or just own a business period. In professional leagues, every player wants to win a world championship. Especially if it is with the team that drafted them. For artists, they could be trying to make that one painting that sells for hundreds of thousands. Becoming a world-renowned artist might be on their radar. For musical artists, they want their albums to sell. Maybe that means going RIAA gold or platinum. Maybe they want to create the #1 song in the world. For city project planners and non-profit organizations, it is the constant fight to lower poverty rates and hunger. When it comes to individuals, being a role model for the next generation could be a dream. Maybe you want to raise a healthy family and build generational wealth. All of these are fun to talk about. However, the plans are rarely executed. When they are, it requires buying from everyone involved. Which is never guaranteed. Why is all this important? How does this help you? To begin, you know how fast the years pass. The time will pass anyway. Why not push yourself? Why not try to become the best version of yourself? You will either be on your death bed grateful or regretful. Secondly, wishing is not working. You can wish all you want but if you fail to put the work in, nothing will happen. This gives you meaning to after the things you care about. No one is telling you how to chase your dream because it is yours. You have that power. You have the freedom to do whatever it takes to get there. People go through life never seizing the opportunities in front of them. You have the opportunity right now to create the life you visualized. To put it bluntly, you can choose between living a boring life or an extraordinary life. Working forty hours per week in a dead-end job that is not your passion is not the way to live. But this could be a stepping stone to your next venture. Using the money earned from your 9-5 to finance your dreams is mandatory. You might have to put in some overtime to get to that next level. There is nothing wrong with working a 9-5. I want this to be clear to you. Plenty of people are unemployed, so count your blessings as an employee. How will you know if you do not go for it? You will be stuck years later asking the "what if" questions and lining up the "I should've" statements. I do not want this to happen to you. If you dream big, you will also gain more confidence. Something will click in your mind, and you get more ideas in return. The possibilities are endless when you are consistent with your work ethic and attitude. We all want to be something. What are you doing today to become that person? This journey challenges you to be uncomfortable. Know that there will be some ugly stages. The work is not always going to be pretty. How you react to the dark stages will be the deciding factor in your success. While it does not last forever, this process will bring you motivation. Discipline can last forever if you stay laser-sharp. We will now circle back to the act of being realistic. There are pros and cons. The negative side will be established first. The problem with being realistic is the automatic limitations. You limit yourself by thinking on a lower level. Putting yourself in one category, one box can cause you to accept the victim role. A victim mentality will not make you successful. When you think this way, you will come up with endless excuses. Why go after one thousand when you can go after millions? If you can swim in a ten-foot-deep pool, why should you hang in the shallow end? Do not downplay your strengths and do not overlook your weaknesses.

There is a positive side as well. Knowing what is physically impossible and accepting the truth will keep you out of denial. There should be no fabrication of what you can and cannot do. This gives you a black and white answer. You can either do it or you cannot. It is that simple. If you want to go further than this, then you can do what is best to one day reach that milestone. I talked about SMART goals earlier. Specific, measurable, attainable, reasonable, and time-oriented goals. This is the chapter about being reasonable. Not wild, but crazy enough to achieve. A lofty goal, within reason. In realistic goal-setting, you know the barriers and threats. What is in the way of you winning? More often than not it is who we see in the mirror. We are at war with ourselves constantly. The version of you that wants to live in comfort wants to take over. This is why you need to connect to your resources if you have them. If you do not have the resources you need, reach out. I guarantee that there is at least one individual that will be happy to help. They are all around, you just have to search. Make the levels clear. Write down the milestones so you know what you need to work on. If you are starting your fitness journey, make it a ten-level process. Try to do one push-up per workout, then five, then ten. Adjust based on your desired level of difficulty. After a few months, you can move on to using the bar for bench press and other compound lifts. Soon you will be hitting personal records. But when you look back, it all started with one squat, one push-up, or one mile. This goes for any activity. Increase the intensity, adjust, then repeat. This covers the measurable part too. You scale your growth the right way. The direction should be linear. There will be some falls, you are not perfect, but you can strive to be. At the same time, try not to get caught up in perfection. I was first introduced to the SMART goal approach in middle school. We were all handed a sheet of paper with the description of each letter in the acronym. At the end of class, we put it on the front of our binders as a reminder. We had the choice to write down our goals. The most common one was "get better grades." While this is a broad, vague goal, one can still measure this. But it lacks the specifics. Sure it is reasonable because you should want to succeed in school. Unfortunately, everyone does not achieve this. Your worth should not be based on good grades. This is one crucial part of your life when you are forming your opinions. So it would be optimal if you took advice from trusted people. You do not have to agree and say yes to everything. The approach that I was introduced to was reiterated in high school. Not every class covered this, but I set goals for myself throughout each semester. I was not too focused on the result because I learned how to embrace the process. It was not as easy as I make it sound. You will be given options. Distractions will be put in your path without warning. It is your job to respond in a way that lines up with your path. Do not conform to what the world wants you to do. Follow your passions and receive criticism from mentors. Avoid taking the opportunity to learn for granted. We are all students of the game. Just because you are older than most, does not exclude you from learning something new. In the same way, just because you are young does not mean you should refrain from teaching others if you have the ability. When we put our egos to the side we open up ourselves to new paths and opportunities. You need these people in your life. Mutual relationships benefit both parties. When you are on the same page, you do not have to worry about the extra conflict. Naturally, we all have different ideas and can occasionally argue, but that is a part of the process. I mentioned your health many times because it affects everything you do. How you breathe, talk, eat, and move throughout the day. From my experience being sleep deprived, you need to prioritize your rest. Recovery is not only beneficial to the muscles but the mind. Have you ever experienced a good dream? It is an amazing feeling until the alarm goes off. How about lucid dreaming? Some people have experienced at least one lucid dream. An even smaller amount experiences this monthly. For the unfamiliar, this is when you know you are dreaming and you start to control what you see. On average, at the least, you should be getting seven hours of sleep every night. Surprisingly, some people operate better when they get less sleep. There is a short burst of energy until the middle of the afternoon. This is what I call the crash stage. Eyelids get heavy, and it seems like you are fighting for your life to stay awake. This is the consequence. There is also the REM sleep. Short for rapid eye movement. REM sleep is important for the retention of memories and learning in the brain. Everyone could use some proper resting techniques to apply hours before going to bed. You need to set a hard non-negotiable bedtime. If you do not do this, you will wiggle your way out of going to bed. You might have to set a reminder to start winding down. Additionally, you should stop the use of electronics around one to two hours before bed. But if you decide to use them right before bed, then buy some blue light glasses to protect your eyes. Too much blue light at night can keep you awake. This could ruin your sleep schedule. To balance the new bedtime, you need to commit to a similar time every morning. Throughout the week you can wake up earlier. Over the weekend, you can wake up slightly later. Try not to sleep through the day. You cannot get your time back, so use it wisely. Put your health first. During your tougher weeks, it is important to rest. Having an effective sleep schedule will help you more in the long run. This is a system that will never stop. You either get good sleep or you do not. Another strategy is stretching. Static stretching, meaning you are holding one position for more than a few seconds. This opens you up and slows your heart rate down. The perfect combination if you want quality sleep. If you are like me, then you enjoy snacking before bed. This is not a time to eat a meal big enough to feed a family. Use this time to eat a light healthy snack. When you eat, make sure you leave enough time to digest. For those who are active, this helps their metabolism and appetite when they wake up. If you are looking to lose weight or just maintain, eating right throughout the day is good enough. It is okay to go to bed hungry. As long as you avoid skipping meals during the day. When I was trying to gain weight in high school, I ate two peanut butter and jelly sandwiches with a glass of milk almost every night. After a while this got boring so I cut it down to one sandwich. Then when I got tired of that, I switched to protein bars and bagels. Understand that this is different for everyone. Some people cannot sleep until they eat, others do not mind going to bed hungry and waiting for the morning. Chamomile tea, almonds, and turkey are just three of many foods that help you sleep. See what works for you. Create the life you dream about. The spark you had as a kid needs to come back if you lost it. Do not lose your spark. The fire inside you is burning today for a reason. Do not put out the flames with your doubt. Go to sleep. Then wake up and work. Most people are drifting through life having never chased their dreams. Imagine how many businesses and great establishments we have missed out on because someone was too afraid to go after them. Picture what your community would look like if we took more risks. While you should think about yourself, think about others. What will others gain from you chasing your dream? Put that into perspective. We all come from different households. What if someone younger than you is in a similar situation? No matter where you go, there will be people looking up to you, old and young. They will be watching how you operate, and how you treat others. Especially when you lose. You could be living through the turning point of your life right now. Realize that you have the power within you. Success has no set expiration date. But do not waste your life on pleasures and comfort. Or you will regret the steps you took on your last day of living. Whether you have children or not, what are you leaving for the next generation? Part of this self-improvement journey is working toward something bigger than yourself. This is where true passion is found. You can be fully present when you are planting seeds. Wherever you are today, you can make an impact. I am sure if you asked around, you could find work. If you want to make a difference, leave your environment better than you found it. When you do this, you inspire others. You pass the torch to the next person. Do not exclude yourself, you are capable of inspiring a large number of people. With the connectivity you have today, you can reach a huge audience on social media. Creating content, passing out flyers, whatever the method is, you can serve. Receiving is fun. When you get the gift you wanted or the award you worked for, you feel worthy. But even without accolades and fame, you are worthy. You should not let anyone in your life who thinks differently. Everyone has gifts and dreams. A small amount executes and an even smaller group changes the world. You are a nobody. You are somebody. Contrary to what the world says, you are a valuable person. Show the world who you are. Is say this to remind you, do not to forget to dream. Do not let life pass you by. You have been brought into this world for a reason. Give your life purpose and meaning by going after your dreams. This is essential to your overall health. Do not take your time for granted. No matter who you are, have some respect for yourself. Dreaming big will unlock many doors that would not be there if you did not take the risk. So take the risk. Jump in the deep end. Tread water and start swimming. Do not forget to dream. I believe in you. Get it done.

CHAPTER 17

SELF DISCOVERY

S elf-discovery at its core is an act of reflection. This is the activity of thinking about your feelings and behaviors. The point of this is to figure out the reasons why you operate this way. This is a lifelong process of gaining a deep understanding of your values and purpose in life. You are discovering who you are. People will ignore this because it forces them to look inward. Living in comfort causes us to look outward. We are freely giving out time, money, and energy to fund a stress-free life. Years of doing this will get you nowhere. You are going against the grain by not taking risks. Without reflection, you do not move, and when you do, it is wasted movement. You need to be able to analyze your life and see where you are projected to go in the next year and beyond. As the driver and passenger in your life, you have the choice to sit back, let life guide you, or take the wheel and go a different direction. You have been around people with low energy. They blame others and appear to have the strength to take charge of their life. But they are mentally weak. Life is not an adventure to them, it is a chore. You need to avoid these people. They will only distract you more and more as the days go by. You are on an important mission. Remember a time in school when the teacher gave back an assignment that was not graded. Maybe this teacher told you to grade your paper as they announced the answers. If you did your work in pencil, you were probably required to grade in pen so that you could not change your answers. You were allowed to evaluate yourself for the first time. Maybe you did good on that test, maybe you failed. Either way, you had to look at your answers. Similarly, you have answers and results that you desire. If you do not hit your target, then you need to find a way to get closer. When you look inward, sometimes you will not like the answers. You have the choice to give yourself a good grade that makes you feel accomplished, or a realistic grade. Depending on how honest you are with yourself, you will either move forward or get stuck in the future. Many people suffer from an identity crisis. This can happen at any age. A period of uncertainty makes an individual insecure about their purpose. It can send you spiraling down a destructive path. You might be familiar with the term mid-life crisis. This is the same as an identity crisis but it happens when you are middle-aged. But you can prevent this from happening. This is not a right of passage when you are in your 40s. People with true passion and drive will rarely experience this. There will always be some level of doubt when you try new things. Fortunately, there are plenty of ways to practice reflection. This is synonymous with being present. Many people need approval from others to get by. You need to be grounded in your values and decisions. While receiving help can be great for beginners, you are responsible in the end. How do you practice self-reflection? You will find that these methods are simple. Meditation is one of them. You know the benefits of breathing exercises. A quick pause in your day to sit with yourself and think is relaxing. You can try journaling. Since it is yours to keep, it does not have to be perfect. It is okay if no one sees what you write. When you question yourself, you can write it down. In moments of great joy, you can write about how grateful you are. When you look back, you can see how much progress you made. You can go back to the list of blessings in your life. Reading content surrounding this topic will also open your mind to new strategies. There is a chance that you will find what you are looking for. One practice might perfectly fit your busy schedule. You are one decision away from a different life. You need to ask yourself a few questions. Are you using your time wisely? We all get the same twenty-four hours each day. We are asleep for a third of that time, more or less. So what are you doing to maximize your most valuable asset? Time is something when wasted, cannot be earned back. The clock continues to move forward. What are you afraid of? You are most likely afraid of failure. This is why people stay at their jobs or in toxic relationships. Anything outside their comfort zone bothers them. The toe the line between a new life and stagnation. Are you currently stressing over uncontrollable things? I have. This is not a phase in life that I recommend. Your mind will make up or find ways to make the world revolve around you. When the weather is not up to your standards, or when traffic is not moving fast enough, you can get irritable. Being stressed throughout the day does not automatically disappear when you go to bed. Those same thought patterns carry over into your sleep and the next day. If you fail to see the signs early, you can be in a chronic miserable state. What are some of the goals you have accomplished so far? If you are properly setting goals and applying a schedule to reach them, then you gain momentum. You are not starting fresh, but you can do it if you need to. Each win will compound onto the next. But if you are in the beginning stage, I suggest you start small. Win in the smaller parts of your life so you can flourish in the bigger parts. To reach a lofty, life-changing goal, you might have to start at ground level. Like dieting, you cannot flip the switch and expect results within the next day or week. After years of eating fried foods and sugary drinks, one salad and a cup of water are not going to fix everything. However, when you start to do your research on what to eat. How nutritious meals can taste good and how they benefit your body. This will give you an idea. You will have a new approach when it comes to losing ten pounds to one hundred or more. How do you feel when you wake up? Do you treat life like a blessing or a curse? When your feet hit the floor you need to be excited about the opportunities that have gone your way and the ones that are to come. Most people who are suffering from identity crises have nothing to look forward to. All they have is their job, a few friends, and instant gratification to go back to. They get discouraged when life is not going their way so they submit to their circumstances. Start the morning with gratitude. How do you do this? Gratitude journaling is a simple exercise that can be done as often as you like. But you can also reach out to friends and family. These are the people you are grateful to have in your life. Maybe it is someone random who did something nice for you. The patient worker took back your wrong order and gave you a new meal. Old friends that you have not seen in years who are interested in where you are now. When you truly sit down for some time and think about it, there are many people and parts of your life to be thankful for. This is why you need to keep a journal or save notes on your phone. The list of what you are grateful for is always changing. If you are in school, the beginning of the year is a blessing. Friends you have not seen in months and your favorite teachers are there. On the last day, you are grateful for getting through another year with your friends. No matter what it looked like, you reached the end. All you can do is appreciate those who supported you and helped you get to the next grade or graduation. What do you need to change about yourself? We all have tendencies that might hurt us in the long run. What are yours? Maybe it is your attitude. One of the many parts of your life that you can control. If this is bad, everything else will be the same. When you have a bad attitude, you repel positive people. You show no interest in new opportunities because it does not feel right. Or you are too lazy to try because you do not want to be below average at anything. Start every day with positivity. Once you get out of bed, take a deep breath and attack the day. Choose one thing to be grateful for when you wake up. Think about that thing during the day. When bad things happen throughout your day, remember you have plenty to be grateful for. A changed mindset will put you in the best position to be successful. The majority of people lack a growth mindset. You need to cultivate one. If you already have one, strengthen it. You will need it when you go through storms. What do you want others to remember about you? When you take your last breath, there are numerous things that people will say about you. If you were active in your community and served others, some will say you had a great heart. For those that gave it all they had in the workplace, your colleagues will talk about your work ethic. Depending on how well you treated others, hopefully, there are nice things said. It is hard for people to forget how you made them feel. I do not want you to fixate on death. It will happen to all of us, some earlier than others. I want you to realize that you live every day, not once. You have the opportunity to make a difference. If you truly want the life you talk about, the one you obsess over, then you are going to have to change your habits. Aligning everything you do to the path of your dreams is hard. Every day is a fight. But think about what you would look like in the future. Imagine how amazing you would feel if you took that one risk. The sadness and disappointment in your older years are not worth it. You cannot afford to miss opportunities. When they are right in front of your face, you have to reach out and take them. What will people remember about you? It is better to be a person who died chasing their dreams than one who never tried at all. Like I said before, the time will pass anyway. In the next few years, you will see who has been working. The separation will be there. You need to pick what side you want to be on in the future. As long as you are actively chasing your dream, you will be there before you know it. When you get there, you work your hardest to stay there. Try not to become satisfied when you reach your desired level. Individuals that think like this do not mind staying in their position. If their goal was to make six figures and they get there, they do nothing to earn more. They avoid learning new skills because that would make them a beginner again. They have already made it in their minds. So they decide to entertain their pleasures by faking their image. The focus is on looking successful. They spend their money on liabilities like cars, designer clothing, and other items. This is all bought so they can flex. But sooner or later their money runs out. They look at all their investments and see that there is nothing to get back. Instead of learning a new skill or exploring their passions, they sit still. Sudden change is what these people are not used to. They are not prepared for the unexpected because they spent their time chasing pleasure. You need to venture out. I suggest you connect to your roots. Go as far back as you need to. There are resources online and people in your family that will tell you about your ancestors. You can find out what country they are from and how they got here. With this, you can also get information about family history as far as health goes. The diseases and causes of death in your family tree can help you live a healthier life. While you cannot pick your genetics, you can decide what you eat and drink. If you want to go deeper, look for the generational curses. Or if you are fortunate enough, look at the forms of generational wealth. What assets, if any, were passed down to your family members? Is there a trust fund? This is uncommon for most families, but you never know. If your family is not rich, and you want them to be, then it is up to you to go for it. Planning for future generations is not easy. But it will be worthwhile when you look back. Where is your family today? Maybe every generation is spread out across the United States. Or overseas. Either way, you must connect with them. With the accessibility of social media, you can find them in a couple of seconds from the search bar. You can also call them. Talking on the phone is a bit more personal than back and forth text messages. If you are old school, you can send them a letter. This is an even higher level of personal connection. They know that you took the time to write the letter and reach out. Especially if sending a text message is the easier route. Ask them how they are doing. Drive or fly to them. If you have the means, visit them as much as you can. See why and how your family operates the way they do. You will experience similar methods of parenting. Without a doubt, your relatives will have different opinions. The way they live is a direct reflection of their life growing up. Each person has their own set of values that they apply to daily life. Whether those values are good or not is up to you to decide. This will give you clarity. It is in your best interest to keep an open mind. This goes for anything in life. Hopefully, your family situation, no matter how prestigious or lowly, should motivate you to do better; go harder. Perhaps you can work toward leaving something of value for those after you Property, stocks, cash, and companies are common examples. Believe it or not, this is bigger than you. Once you realize that, you can go through the toughest trials that life throws at you. You do not have to be alone when it comes to discovering yourself. Explore. Go into unfamiliar communities. What I mean by this is groups and organizations that fit your passion. The ones that you have not worked in. You will meet new people and make connections. Your purpose has the potential to be found there. Then one day, you can be the next person to help someone use their passions for long-lasting work. In these new experiences, learn how to reflect. Fully immerse yourself. What are you thinking about? How are you feeling in the present moment? What does it look like? How are you reacting to your environment? If you do not like your environment, then change it. The least you can do is temporarily move to a new place to work on your passions. Not a different city, state, or country. But if you can afford it, go right ahead. I am referring to a new place within your location. A library, coffee shop, or outside on your deck. It could be a country club, office space, park, or outside on your deck. If you are more productive in these spaces, then you need to keep going there. Optimize your place of work so that you can reach your full potential. Maybe the one thing stopping you from getting to the top is your environment. If it is not positively serving you, you need to leave. If you cannot leave, make the most of it right now. When you stay consistent and committed, you will not be stuck there forever. Even though that place has become a part of your identity, it is okay to disconnect for a while. Give yourself time to process who you are. You have the power. If you want an activity that will give you quick results, then try taking a personality test. There are eight categories that a person has the potential to fall in. The type of personality will be defined by four of those eight. There are sixteen different personalities that you can find yourself in. The first two types are extroverts and introverts. Extroverts get their energy from being around people. They like fast-paced activities and multitask often. Introverts enjoy working alone and work on tasks one at a time. They enjoy activities at a steady pace. Depending on your energy, you are either a sensor or an intuitive type. Sensors stick to the facts and use common sense. If they have prior knowledge, they use it to solve problems. Intuitive types think conceptually. They are more creative when looking for solutions. The next two are self-explanatory. Thinkers appreciate honesty and consistency. They take a logical approach when making decisions. The option with more pros than cons is typically chosen. Though, that can apply to most people. Of course, you want more possible benefits than setbacks. But that is how thinkers operate. Feelers are a bit more sensitive. They use their values and think about others more than themselves. The question they ask themselves is, "How will this help others?" The last two types are judgers and perceivers. Judgers are organized. They are okay with following rules and value being prepared. When it comes to plans they prefer sticking to them, not deviating from them. Perceivers are more flexible when plans are established. They are on the side of spontaneity and like to explore their options. Many different websites provide personality tests with instant results. Some of them let you get a copy of it through text or email. There are many rare types like INFJ, ENTJ, and INTJ. But whatever your results, you will be given strengths and weaknesses. Some of which, you already know. How do you move forward after getting your results? Read the qualities, and how you operate. Look for detailed descriptions of how relationships with others work. Most tests will give you tips on how to use your personality in your work and social life. Whether you are a student or deep into your adult life, it is okay to get feedback from people you trust. They see you from a different perspective. They are not around you all day.

They do not know what you are doing when no one is watching. But they know how you act in social settings. How you react when things go wrong around them is what they remember. If you trust that they are authentic, they will give you feedback that is not faked. What you need to hear are the bad habits you commit. If I was seeking feedback, I would not want anyone to lie to me and tell me everything is good. As great as it feels, it will not help me. In the same way, it will not help you either. You need constructive criticism. When you go off the trail, you need people to call you out and get back on track. These people can choose what to focus on when you spend time with them. It is fairly easy to tell who the extroverts and introverts are in the group. When there is a project due, sensors and intuition might clash. If you face an ethical dilemma, thinkers and feelers might argue too. Thinkers are more objective in the way they attack problems. Feelers tend to put their emotions into their problems more than most. Remember, wherever you land on the list, you matter. You can add value to your environment by using your strengths. The best tactic is communicating with people opposite of you. This is where true growth is, in uncomfortable environments. You do not have to agree with everything someone says, but if you can work well with them, great things happen. When you are aware of your tendencies you can cut back on the bad ones. In times of conflict, you will be emotionally intelligent, which is a quality many people lack. There are other ways to raise your level of emotional intelligence. In stressful situations, you need to stay calm and manage. You need to be able to express your emotions and not suppress them. Take ownership. Take care of your body throughout the day. Find time to relax. You need to take this journey of finding yourself seriously. If you try to speed up the process, you will not enjoy the results. I understand that there are points in your life when you feel lost. This is when you should work on your passions. Doing what you love will bring you great joy. Trust yourself. The individuals from your past will notice. Some people in your life put you into one category. They believe you are still the old version of yourself. The one with no ambition that was down for anything. In their minds, they associate you with the destructive activities you did in the past. They do not fully recognize this new version of you. On your journey, they will try to pull you down to their level. Instead of being inspired, they wallow in their envy, looking for the next person to derail. Do not fall into their trap. Sometimes you have to leave people where they are so they can understand where you want to be. They might not ever come back into your life, but that should be a risk you are willing to take. When you set those boundaries for yourself, it will be easier to leave them behind. The more you associate with the negative, the less progress you make. Be intentional. In this current moment, what do you value about yourself? Maybe you want to serve people but do not know how, that is okay. You should look for volunteering opportunities in your community. If you get your energy from being alone, then do something for yourself. Treat yourself to a day of rest, or an activity that you enjoy with no one around. If you love what you are doing, you will make time to continue that feeling. I know that there is a great amount of weight on your shoulders when you are discovering yourself again. There was a time in your life when you had no worries and every day felt pleasant. Honestly, that is a lie. You are fooling yourself if you believe every day will be peaceful and worry-free. However, worrying about everything will break you down emotionally. You are in control of yourself. What you let in is what you let out. The results you get are a combination of the work you put in. So there is no reason not to use your strength and gifts. I want to let you know that your mistakes do not define you. Each day you wake up is an opportunity to detach from your old self. If you are trying to discover yourself, chances are you lost yourself previously. This is okay. You are making an effort that is worth your time. Doubting your judgment will hurt you. Stick to being decisive. Stand tall in your decisions. Even if you make a mistake. You might think this is selfish due to your childhood and beliefs now, but it is okay to put yourself first. Know your worth. You are not an ordinary person. The life of average people is not what you want to live. Believe that you are here for a reason. To sit around all day and not go after your dreams is a selfish act. People like this give into temptation and bad routines, then wonder why they are stuck. At the beginning of your pursuit of discovering yourself, there is lots of questioning. When it comes to making decisions, I do not want you to second-guess yourself. What I mean by questioning is your current ways. The way you think, speak and act. Chances are, you are not where you want to be, but you are getting closer. This is not about perfection, it is about consistency. Where are you using your energy? Who do you feel drained around? Who motivates you? How do you react when other people experience success? Your character matters. Through this time, you need to have an abundance mindset. An individual with this mindset believes there are enough resources to go around. Success is attainable for everyone. They say, "If others can win, I can too." People who look at life with abundance look for opportunities daily. On their worst days, they still know they can win. They are optimistic and work well with others. An abundance mindset can take you far. You can inspire others to do the same. Some people need extra motivation and you can be the one to bring that energy. This makes a big difference in the workplace. People need reasons to wake up in the morning, especially when they are discouraged. An abundance mindset will help you see endless possibilities. You will get creative with your solutions too. Everyone who works has the opportunity to grow. This is not a solo mission. You need a support system. It does not matter how many people you have either. You are discovering yourself by serving others and capitalizing on your skills. If you feel called to a certain organization, then accept it. Remember that it is okay to feel. Drawing near toward your passion feels better than wondering. Have undeniable effort. Keep knocking on the door and it will soon open. In the dark times, other doors will close so new ones can open. You are free to pick more than one option. When you find that one place, you will know. A new sense of urgency will be obtained. When you are willing to go through criticism from haters and supporters, the lessons are worth it. You are equipped with experience. What inspired me to write this book was my friends and family. I saw the way they lived. Some of them felt like they had no purpose. A few of them did not know where they were going in life. They were just drifting, making little to no moves at all. I wanted to talk to all of them at once but that was not easy. So I started writing. This is my message to them. I am also teaching myself in the process. When you decide to do something big, like write a book, make music, sell art, or services; you have to look inward. You have to make sure you want to do this. If you plan on being consistent in your efforts, then you need to be all in. You might need to question yourself. Is this what you want? Receiving approval from your loved ones is great, but you need to approve yourself. These people will not always be there to make decisions for you. Having the strength to be decisive and know exactly what you want is not average. The average people in this world are not thinking for themselves.

They say yes to everything because they are afraid of losing people. This is where the scarcity mindset runs. This person believes there is not enough to go around, so they hoard. Some of the things they hoard are resources, success, and even friends. They believe they are not worthy of love, money, and success. Unfortunately, it takes time to get this person on the other side of thinking. They are pessimistic. If they are not perfect, they fall apart. Think of a person in your life with a scarcity mindset. How do they act when someone close to them wins? They are probably jealous of their success. It would take a miracle to get an amazing opportunity for them. These people are hard to work with because they have no hope. They spend time making sure they get their success without giving credit to anyone. The opposite of a scarcity mindset is found in gratitude. As you can imagine, this person is not grateful. Not even for the little things. They wake up in a fear of losing it all. So they hold their phone tightly and money. If these people are your friends, it is hard to leave them. You know you have the power to change them. But being around them feels like a chore. It is like you are babysitting. They are codependent. Give them advice by sharing your methods of practicing gratitude. If they truly want to change, then they will listen. They might not understand what you are doing now, but they will later. We have all fallen short of our goals. Maybe you fought your temptation instead of fleeing from it. Nobody is perfect. As long as you have a pulse, there is time to rediscover yourself. This is going to take some searching. You are going to have to be vulnerable for some time. Identify your thought patterns throughout the day. Your attitude is everything. Your mindset guides you. People will know how committed you are based on your words and body language. Try to think of multiple solutions to your problems. Seek new opportunities because they are out there. Make new connections. Increase your network to your liking. Stay strong. Allow yourself to feel. Do not push your feelings to the side. Avoiding your passions will halt your progress. Think of discovering yourself as an experiment. You are exploring your options and seeing how you react to them. Use an abundance mindset to your advantage. Imagine what you can do! Get excited! This is the life we are talking about! You can experience great things on your journey of self-discovery. Have fun. Embrace it. Stay ready.

CHAPTER 18

NEXT STEPS

The first chapter in this book covered your journey. You learned how to embrace your journey. Too many people get caught up in the comparison game. We might have similar goals, but not everyone is doing the same things to reach them. Depending on your family situation, you either have an efficient support system or lack one. I advise you to compare yourself only to the person you were yesterday. Not anyone else. If you cannot see the difference between who you were in the past compared to today, then you need to get to work. The journey challenges you. Sometimes you are humbled by those who are doing better than you. This should excite you because you have the potential to get there too. You benefit more from taking action than talking about it. Anybody can talk, but few get the job done. People who fail to put the work in are usually left miserable. Most of us who are trying to succeed are after similar goals. What are you doing that is different? What ordinary thing are you doing better than most? Be intentional and different. Celebrate the small wins in private. Learn from the losses in private. People begin at different start lines, but that does not disqualify you from winning. Maybe they got a head start. This is out of your control. Like the gym, for example. People show up with different goals. Nobody looks the same. As a beginner, you might think that you do not have what it takes to lift that weight, lead that project, or be that figure. But you can. First, you have to believe that you can. No amount of motivation is worth it if you have no confidence in yourself. In the next chapter, you were introduced to the harmful effects of staying in your comfort zone. Staying in your comfortable spot for years will harm you. There is a high chance that it will kill you. From my understanding, you do not want to be stuck in one spot. You crave the intensity when it comes to chasing your dreams. If you are like me, then you want better for yourself and your loved ones. We are blinded by our comfort because it is so accessible. Degenerative activities are advertised to us in a glorified way. Smoking; was once advertised to minors and still is through outside pressure to fit in. Now there are campaigns to stop this. Every puff takes away some years of your life. No one wants to be bound to an oxygen tank, or stuck in their home forever. Drinking is also popular. At parties, it is like there is a competition to see who can black out the fastest. The costs in the short and long run should make you rethink. What you want out of life requires you to leave your comfort zone. You do not grow in comfort. You grow in discomfort. If all your circle does is participate in these activities, you need a new circle. It is not worth your life. I challenge you to seek discomfort daily. I want this to become a part of your routine. Most people will not participate because they are fearful. Their first mistake is caring what others think. How are you stepping outside your comfort zone today? Spend some time thinking about that. I will admit, this is ugly at first. The natural habit is to get as comfortable as possible so you will not get hurt. But true growth is found in doing the opposite. You will feel vulnerable. But I promise you it will be worth it in the end. Maybe you will find your purpose outside of this zone. When you have no purpose, you have no direction. As a result, you will most likely fall back to old ways. If you think you cannot improve, you are mistaken. This is the fixed mindset that ruins a large number of people. You need a growth mindset. Anything you want to do you can accomplish. With dedication and consistency, you will hit your marks. Take learning a new language. You start with the basics. Once you have that down then you move to the intermediate level. After you cross that milestone, you go to the expert level. Before you know it, you will be fluent. Then you will find ways to raise the bar even higher. Someone good at serving others should use those skills to make an impact in their community. For the most part, they do it for themselves. It makes them feel complete. To grow as a person, you need to do what you say you are going to do. When it is all said and done, you are only cheating yourself. Not holding yourself to your word will make you look less authentic. People will not trust you if you continue to act this way. This could be your first time experiencing success. You might feel like a fraud. Going back to imposter syndrome. We all get it. Even with a sense of urgency, it is okay to take the pressure off. Mistakes are a part of the process. I believe the result is much sweeter when the odds are not in your favor. Face your fear of failure and rejection. If you do not, you will be targeted. Life will challenge you either way so it would help if you embraced it. At some point, you will have to lead. Not only yourself but your family, colleagues, and friends. Despite your limiting beliefs, you can be a leader. When it is time to step up, you need to have faith. All of the topics above contribute to you reinventing yourself. I will ask you once again. Who do you want to be? Where do you want to be? Visualize that amazing life you want to live. Try to avoid destination addiction syndrome. Choose to be happy now, but not satisfied. However, the reality is, that you will not be energized daily. There were times when I questioned my ability. I had to intentionally look in the mirror. After journaling, deep thinking, and consulting with my friends; I got back up. What I needed to do was leave the toxic people in my life. I was consuming their negativity and almost lost myself in the process. Many people will be placed in your life to test you. They are there to see if you will slip up. I want the best for you. It is in your best interest to surround yourself with supportive people. Those that are fully present. They are the best people to be around. Who are you listening to? What are you allowing into your life? You cannot agree with everything. This is why having values and morals are important. It is your compass. Due to your upbringing, you might have adopted some bad values. It was not your job in your early years to teach yourself, but it is your responsibility now. You might have to unlearn some things that you were forced to learn as a child. Take inventory of your thought patterns. These lead you through your habits. You will not be a changed person overnight. This is a continuous process. Soon, you will not have to think about it, you will just do it. Some believe self-improvement is a pointless topic. But it is fairly relevant as there are more ways to profit in society today. We need to be able to adapt to our surroundings. If you are stuck in the past, you have no time to enjoy the present. Life will pass you by the lazier you become. Your effort is one of many things you can control. Sometimes you will be exhausted. Fortunately, you do not have to solve every problem at once. You break it down into steps. Then you calculate the risks. Setting SMART goals will allow you to see what is attainable. In some cases, it will be trial by fire, but most of it will be gradual. Once you master the gradual process, you start progressively overloading. Maybe this is spending an extra few minutes to an hour a day focusing on one task. Make the schedule clear. You can complete different tasks on certain days. Do not overwhelm yourself by doing the same thing every day. Your lacking areas will be neglected. This will show in your work and relationships. Be the driver of your life. Understand that if you want to change, this is going to take all of you. Holding back and coasting will not give you the desired results. Everything that I was good at, I brought all the energy I had. Working on my weaknesses was not as exciting. But I learned more from those experiences. Sometimes you have to go through losses to prepare you for big wins. Trust me. Remember what dreaming big can do to you. You need to think bigger. What do you want to accomplish? What do you want others to accomplish? Similar to your support system, you can be the supportive friend to someone else. This is iron sharpening iron. The mutual relationships in your life will benefit you. I have friends that I have been close to for years. Every single one of them provided value to me, and I did the same for them. Most of them did not come from the best home or environments, yet they still go after their dreams. This is inspiring to me to this day. I value the relationships because I believe they will always stay intact. Some of them make music, others are winning in sports, a few have started families. Seeing them succeed makes me happy. Especially when I know what they had to go through to get there. The company you keep will either push you to the next level, or pull you down. Go back to the ego chapter. You make your presence known in the lives of others. There is nothing wrong with have a strong sense of self. Having more confidence than others can help you move faster. You can assist others with finding their confidence too. Pride says, "I am always right." Ego says, "I am good enough. I do not need to improve." These are the voices in your head competing for attention. The more you feed into them, the harder it will be to recognize your weaknesses.

When I would accumulate certain levels of success, especially when I was younger, I was quickly humbled. For the teams I have played for, the same thing happens. You start peaking, you get to a certain point, get comfortable, then you plateau. The plateau leads to a decline. The success gets to your head. You cannot let this happen. I am not telling you to downplay your achievements. Celebrate your wins. So what are the next steps? What does this mean for you? How will you grow in discomfort? First, I want you to look at every part of your life. I want you to look at the family and friends you currently have. Be objective. This is your chance to use logic. Weight out the pros and cons of your relationships with these people. How have they helped you? In what ways did they hurt you? If they hurt you, figure out why you stay around them. Maybe it is because you have known them for so long that you are afraid of letting go. A part of you loves them. The memories shared and the rest of the history you have is still meaningful to you. But is it worth it to stay with the negative people? You already know the answer deep down. I want you to identify those that lack direction. Trying to save everyone else in your life will leave you exhausted. You will be drained of your resources. On a plane, in the unlikely event of an emergency, the flight attendants tell you to put your oxygen mask on first before helping others. Why is that? You put you mask on first because without your resources and needs being met, oxygen, you do not have the power to take care of others. You cannot pour from an empty cup. Do not let these people tell you that it is wrong to want better for yourself. If you are the smartest or richest person out of the group, you need a new group. People below your level do not have the experience. They lack the knowledge needed to guide you on your path. Maybe you need to sit down with them. Appreciate the good things they have done, but let them know how you feel. You cannot let your emotions get the best of you. But if this person has done nothing good to you, then you can cut them off. They have taken enough from you. One thing that is not mandatory, is explaining yourself. They do not have to understand your vision. After all, it is your vision. Protect it. Some people in your life do not deserve to hear it. Who do you share good news with? Are they genuinely happy for you? Or are they jealous? The people that constantly downplay your success should not be around you. They seem to never be happy for you. Since they put themselves first, their ego drives them to negativity. When their friends win, they are envious. So they do what is in their nature; dragging others down to their level. When you are playing a video game, leaning a new skill, or pursuing a new career, the objective is to level up. No one is telling you to level down. If you do not get better, you stay in the same place. When you stay in the same place, there is a chance of you getting worse. The reality is, in the darkness, when you are by yourself. When life is hitting you from all directions and there is no exit in sight, all you have is your mindset. The values that you accumulate over time are important. The relationships you commit to that are positive will bring you success beyond your imagination. In all honesty, no one has the responsibility to save you. But when you are at your lowest, their true colors will show. Attack your problems, the things you do not like about yourself, with the idea that no one is coming to save you. However, it is okay to aso fr help on the way. In isolation, without regulation, we do not grow as members in our communities. Take a minute each day to visualize the life you want. Just for one minute, look into your dream future. Write down your goals then pair them with plans. Aggressively pursue and do not look back. Give yourself time to prepare, then execute. This is not going to be instant. It might be a few months or years before you see results. In the mean time, I want you to be patient. But you need to be working. Sitting on the couch and scrolling through social media all day will not help you one bit. There will be short burst of motivation that make you want to run through walls. This is all good, but you cannot rely on motivation. In fact, you might be motivated in the beginning. Yet it will not carry you all the way. Therefore, you need to figure out your why. Why are you doing this? Why did you decide to enter that field? Besides yourself, who are you doing this for? Purpose is found in the actions we do to attain a goal or objective. You know deep down what you have to do. You cannot predict our success, but you can take the steps today to get closer and closer. Maybe you were told lies as a child. Or you were influenced by the worst types of people. Somewhere along the way somebody told you that you could not make it. Maybe they said your dream was too lofty. Additionally, this person or the group of people were threatened by your potential. So they left your discouraged. It is not uncommon to be surorounded by them. When you chose to open up, they shot down your idea. For a few moments, you forgot who you were. Then you started searching for validation by participating in destructive activities. Maybe you isolated because you felt unworthy. Whatever the case, you were broken. A part of you might still be broken today. We all have different pains. I will not compare mine to yours because we are not living in the same shoes. As you go on your journey, you will meet people who have been in similar situations. The bonds you create will propel you forward. This is just one part of your personal development. Your growth is a combination of your dreams, identity, community, and how you put in the work. The truth is, you can read all the books you can about discipline and motivation. None of the content will be beneficial to you if you refuse to take action. I want the best for you. Many people waste their opportunities just so they can get an ounce of comfort. Meditate, take inventory of your friends; evaluate everything you do. But try to reduce your stress in the process. Optimize your routine. Remove anything and anyone that does not serve you in a positive way. You are not your past. Do the activities that force you to stay present. Bring your full self. Look introspectively. It is amazing to see what individuals can accomplish when they decide to seek discomfort. Be extraordinary. To conclude, I want you to remember the methods I shared with you. But most of all, I want you to believe in yourself, even when no one else does. Keep taking steps to live your dream life. You've got this. Go forth and excel.

Printed in the United States
by Baker & Taylor Publisher Services